hotels • restaurants • shops • spas • resorts • galleries • bars

singaporechic

hotels • restaurants • shops • spas • resorts • galleries • bars

singaporechic

To obtain preferential rates and amenities at the hotels
featured in *Singapore Chic*, please register online at:
www.thechicseries.com
info@thechicseries.com

hotels • restaurants • shops • spas • resorts • galleries • bars

singapore chic

text aun koh • susan lcong

ARCHIPELAGO PRESS

executive editor
melisa teo
editors
candice lim • melissa ramos
designer
lisa damayanti
production manager
sin kam cheong
sales and marketing director
antoine monod
sales and marketing manager
new bee yong

editions didier millet pte ltd
121 telok ayer street, #03-01
singapore 068590
email: edm@edmbooks.com.sg
website: www.edmbooks.com

©2006 editions didier millet pte ltd

Printed in Singapore

isbn: 981-4155-74-8

1		5		13			19
	3		6	11	12	14	
2	4		7				20
		9			16	17	
8		10	15			18	21

COVER CAPTIONS:

1: StraitsKitchen at Grand Hyatt Singapore.
2: Floral bath at Spa Botanica at The Sentosa Resort & Spa.
3, THIS PAGE AND PAGE 6: *Chic décor at the New Majestic Hotel.*
4: A bird resting in a park.
5: A devotee carrying a vel kavadi during the Thaipusam festival.
6: The Istana.
7: Fine dining at Saint Julien Le Restaurant.
8: The modern Lounge Bar at Il Lido.
9: Durians in Geylang.
10: Stylish threads at Balenciaga.
11: Oriental setting at My Humble House.
12, PAGE 8 AND 9: *The Merlion with shades.*
13: Satay.
14: The Fullerton Hotel Singapore.
15: Glass dome of the Esplanade—Theatres on the Bay.
16: Shadow of a shopper.
17 AND OPPOSITE: *Colourful windows of a restored shophouse.*
18: Hip accommodation at Hotel 1929.
19: The financial district overlooking the Singapore River.
20: Sculpture detail of the Victorian-style Tan Kim Seng Fountain.
21: Soothing hues and cosy ambience at the pierside kitchen&bar.

PAGE 2: Funky wall painting at the New Majestic Hotel.

contents

Malaysia

Strait of Johor

Pasir Ris East

Jurong Strait

Pandan Strait

singapore**by**constituencies

singapore**by**chapters

Around the Island

Chinatown + Arab Street + Little India

Orchard Road

Civic District

Chinatown + Arab Street + Little India

Strait of Singapore

introduction

destination singapore

Singapore today is one of the well-heeled travellers' favourite destinations for business and leisure. Despite naysayers who decry the Lion City as a soulless and boring place, most residents and visitors know Singapore for what it really is—the most cosmopolitan city in Southeast Asia. As the Singapore Tourism Board declared with its "Uniquely Singapore" campaign, Singapore stands out in so many ways from other countries in its region. It is a city of remarkable contrasts that is able to balance the modern and traditional without one encroaching on the other. Here, one can stroll down one of the world's most celebrated and chic shopping streets to check out favourite European brands in boutiques housed in temples of glass and steel; and just as quickly step out to the city's conservation areas and explore century-old Buddhist and Hindu temples.

business and the economy

Singapore is known to the world as an economic miracle. It is a country with no natural resources that gained independence only in the 1960s. Today, it is a prosperous, modern city. It is the favoured location of international companies that have a regional base in Asia.

With a GDP of US$120.9 billion, Singapore has often been singled out as having the best business environment and the best business infrastructure in Asia. It is a country that seriously supports intellectual property protection, business transparency and free market competition, which make it attractive to foreign business and investment.

safety and efficiency

It is also a city of remarkable efficiency—which might explain why so many detractors call it boring. But efficiency is not boring. It is, at least for the global nomad, the businessman, the politician and the family on their first holiday in years,

THIS PAGE: The flow of traffic is smooth and orderly even during rush hour.

OPPOSITE: The cityscape by the Singapore River is especially mesmerising at night, with dazzling lights from The Fullerton Hotel and Esplanade— Theatres on the Bay.

a welcome relief. Singapore is also safe, which again doesn't mean it's boring. One can go out dancing with friends at Singapore's top club, Zouk, and still be able to walk back to the hotel at 3 am without a worry in the world.

national pastimes

For most travellers, Singapore is noteworthy for two things: shopping and eating. The jet-setting fashionista and smart shopper will not want for things to buy because there is a diverse range of merchandise, from hard-to-find luxury goods to traditional handicrafts, to keep shopaholics very happy.

Similarly, eating is a joy in this foodies' paradise. From haute cuisine in fine dining restaurants to Asian street food in hawker centres, there is more than enough variety across styles and price ranges to keep everyone satisfied.

Singapore is also beginning to build a reputation for its nightlife and parties. Annual club events like Zoukout! in Sentosa island are attended by more than 15,000 dance fanatics. With some of the best hotels, boutiques, bars, clubs, restaurants, and spas in Asia, Singapore is a popular holiday destination that draws more than 7 million visitors a year.

history

One of the amazing things about this 699-sq km (270-sq mile) island nation is that it's gone from colonial port to global village in less than 50 years. From a sleepy backwater with reportedly less than 150 people, it became a modern metropolis with 4 million inhabitants in less than 200 years.

Three individuals figure prominently in Singapore's history: Sang Nila Utama, Sir Thomas Stamford Raffles and Lee Kuan Yew.

According to legend, Utama, a Sumatran prince and the first king of the Malays, was the founder of Singapore. He was also the man who gave Singapore its name, renaming the island previously known as Temasek "Singa Pura". According to the *Malay Annals*, which records the establishment of the Malacca Sultanate and covers over 600 years of the Malay Peninsula's history, Utama discovered Temasek during a sailing expedition. Upon landing on the island whose white, sandy beaches attracted him, Utama spotted a beast with a black head, a red tawny body and a white breast, which ran away at the sight of him and his men. Utama saw the creature—a lion—as an omen of good fortune, and decided to stay on the island.

He renamed the area Singa Pura, which is Sanskrit for "Lion City". Utama reportedly ruled Singa Pura for 48 years and heralded a golden age on the island. New archaeological evidence has led many to believe that this golden age did, in fact, occur in the 14th century. Whether or not it was under Utama's rule, written records and evidence point to a thriving, cosmopolitan society with diplomatic and trading links with both South Asia and East Asia around that time. However, the kingdom declined during the 15th century, and Singapore had all but disappeared.

Over the next three centuries, Singapore became little more than a footnote in history books, mentioned only as being a home base for pirates, then as part of continuing struggles of the Thai and Javanese empires, and later on of European powers seeking dominance of the region.

In the early 19th century, Sir Thomas Stamford Raffles, a British Lieutenant-
Governor with the British East India Empire had read the *Malay Annals* and decided
to, as he put it, "return the ancient glory" of the civilisation that had made Singapore
a great nation in the past. He first arrived in Singapore in 1819. Recognising its
strategic geographic location, he quickly made a treaty with the Malay rulers of the
island and established Singapore as a British port for free trade. Although he is, to this
day, considered the founder of Singapore, Raffles soon left the island, leaving
Colonial William Farquhar in charge of the difficult task of running and developing the
new territory. Raffles did, however, have a hand in much of the new territory's urban
development. In fact, evidence of some of his guidelines, such as segregated areas
for various ethnic communities, is still present today. Singapore rapidly grew from a
fishing village to an important international trading zone, overshadowing Malacca
and Penang, its nearby sister ports within the Straits Settlements. Its population

skyrocketed, growing by over 700 per cent between 1819 and 1869. Most of these new immigrants were Chinese. In 1867, the Straits Settlements, which Singapore was a part of, became a British Crown Colony. When the Suez Canal was opened in 1869, Singapore became even more geographically important for the British Empire. Over the next 60 years or so, life in Singapore was, especially for the expatriates and Chinese tycoons, a time of peace, growth and prosperity for many.

World War II changed things forever. It was something that was thought impossible. Singapore was taken by the Japanese. Worse, Singapore was invaded and defeated in just one week. The Japanese Occupation, during which Singapore was called "Syonan" or light of the south, was brutal and vicious. It was during this period that the local Chinese, Malay and Indian population made a startling realisation: the British were not indestructible, nor were they perfect. This insight surfaced and made a huge impact after the war was over.

ABOVE: Recognising its geographical advantage, Sir Stamford Raffles transformed Singapore into a trading port.
OPPOSITE: Today, PSA Singapore Terminals is the world's busiest port and a global leader in the ports and terminals business.

...more than 85 per cent of Singaporeans own homes.

When World War II ended in 1945, Singapore returned to civil administration as a Crown Colony. However, the people of both Singapore and Malaysia now wanted self-rule. A long, drawn-out handover took place, and self-government for Singapore was finally attained in 1959. That year, the People's Action Party (PAP), led by a young Cambridge-educated lawyer named Lee Kuan Yew, won a majority of the seats. In 1963, Singapore merged with Malaysia but was separated in 1965 because of political differences. The image of Lee Kuan Yew, the man most synonymous with Singapore's success, crying upon the announcement of expulsion remains one of the most powerful scenes in Singapore's modern political history.

modern Singapore

Few countries in the world have grown as quickly, modernised as rapidly, and had to adapt as drastically as Singapore has since its independence and birth as a republic in 1965. The man behind much of this development is Singapore's first Prime Minister, Lee Kuan Yew. A tough but brilliant leader who won the support of equally intelligent and passionate nationalists, Lee could see Singapore's natural limitations as far back as the late 1950s. To overcome the odds, Lee built his government along a Platonic ideal: in *The Republic*, Plato wrote that a perfect city-state should be run by a philosopher-king and the guardian class, whose right to rule is legitimised by the rest of society.

To this day, no opposition party has ever fielded enough people to win majority of the seats in Parliament. The PAP, which has dominated the elections since 1959, uses election periods and the annual National Day celebrations to remind Singaporeans of the progress it has achieved. And that, fortunately, has been nothing short of amazing.

Lee's government emphasised stability and productivity. It also regarded transparency and incorruptibility as necessary. National defence, education, housing, infrastructure, civic order, industrialisation, modernisation, tourism and economic development have all been national priorities, each looked after by a team of highly educated civil servants. Since 1965, Singapore's economy has grown by an average

THIS PAGE (CLOCKWISE FROM TOP): Showing support to the soldiers at the National Day Parade; an impressive display of military aviation technology during an Asian Aerospace show; Minister Mentor Lee Kuan Yew—the man behind the development of modern Singapore—and Prime Minister Lee Hsien Loong.

OPPOSITE: Public housing dominates Singapore's skyline in the residential districts.

of 9 per cent each year. Literacy rates are higher than 90 per cent and more than 85 per cent of Singaporeans own homes. Lee and his ministers were also quick to recognise that Singapore needs to be connected to the global economy in order to survive. It must position itself as not just a service provider but also as a major player and a financial hub with investments around the globe.

In 1990, Goh Chok Tong succeeded Lee as Prime Minister. He, in turn, was succeeded by Lee's son, Lee Hsien Loong in 2004. Civil service has made similar efforts to promote younger talent into senior roles, ensuring new blood in the upper echelon of government.

Critics of Lee's policies, however, have often pointed wagging fingers at Singapore's admittedly none-too-stellar human rights record. But as most visitors discover, Singaporeans are hardly living in fear. Majority are in fact quite happy

THIS PAGE: *Skyscrapers in the financial district.*

OPPOSITE: *As a multiracial society, Singaporeans get to enjoy a rich diversity in cultures.*

that they live in an efficient society that is free of problems such as corruption and traffic jams. Many visitors also find that a lot of Singaporeans are extremely outspoken, whether they're loudly boasting of their country's successes or freely griping about the system. The underlying truth about Singapore is that most people have accepted the social contract made with the ruling elite, whom they trust to ensure that the country and its citizens prosper.

people: a mosaic of different cultures

In a statement in 1991, then Prime Minister Goh said that as long as the economy is growing and there is plenty for everybody, people would not fight over small things. But if the pie is shrinking, that will be the real test of whether Singaporeans as a people are cohesive or fragile.

For a small Southeast Asian nation with a population of 4 million, social cohesion may be the one thing that worries the government the most. The local population is made up of 77 per cent Chinese, 14 per cent Malay, 8 per cent Indian. The rest belong to other ethnic groups.

The largest percentage of the country's population is Chinese, most of whom are from southern China. The Hokkiens are the largest group, followed by the Teochews, Cantonese, Hakkas and Hainanese. Each of these groups speak a different dialect and have their own customs, festivals and cuisine. The emphasis on speaking Mandarin, however, has meant that more and more young Singaporeans no longer speak their dialects. The Malays form the second largest group, followed by the Indians. Most Indians in Singapore are from either Tamil Nadu or from Tamil-speaking parts

of Sri Lanka. Tamil, in fact, has become one of the country's four official languages. A unique group that Singapore now recognises as a race are the Eurasians. These people are the descendants of Europeans that came here during the colonial period and married Chinese, Indian or Malay women. Most Eurasians are Christian and are very westernised, but are also quite Asian in that they incorporate Asian customs in western traditions. A Eurasian Christmas dinner, for instance, is just as likely to have curry as it would have a turkey.

Apart from the Eurasians, there is also a group of Straits Chinese, or Peranakans—descendants of Chinese sailors who immigrated to the Straits of Melaka and took Malay brides. Their cuisine, known as Nonya or Peranakan cuisine, is considered by many to be the very best style of local cooking.

The large immigrant and expatriate groups in Singapore come from as far as Indonesia and the United States. This constant influx of new people is helping Singapore become more and more cosmopolitan. Different races live in harmony in this country, whose policy welcomes most foreigners with open arms. What Singapore's leaders want most is for its citizens to be nationalistic—to be proud of being Singaporean and at the same time be proud of their own cultural and racial heritage.

For the young Chinese or Indian boy, this can be confusing as he is repeatedly reminded that he's part of the melting pot, but is forced to study Chinese or Tamil in school as a second language (or what the local educational system refers to as "mother tongue") because of his race. Nonetheless, Singapore's efforts to build a national identity have generally worked. This is especially so for the younger generation, who identify less with their peers in China, India or Malaysia, and readily distinguish themselves as Singaporeans when asked about their origins.

THIS PAGE: The Sri Mariamman temple in Chinatown is known for its ornate gopuram, the tower crowning its entrance.

OPPOSITE (CLOCKWISE FROM TOP): A Taoist priest in a solemn ritual; colourful windows of restored shophouses; home to a variety of faiths and beliefs, Singapore allows for freedom of religion.

different faiths

Singapore is first and foremost an immigrant nation. Despite claims that suggest otherwise, even the Malay population is not indigenous to the island or the peninsula. This multiracial community means that Singapore is home to a variety of faiths and belief systems. A survey taken in 2000 shows 85 per cent of its residents aged 15 years and over adhere to a religious faith or belief. With a population that

is predominantly Chinese, 51 per cent of Singapore's residents are either Buddhist or Taoist. Almost all of the Malays are Muslim, although some are more conservative than others. Fifteen per cent of the population belong to one of Christianity's various denominations, where Protestants outnumber Roman Catholics by at least two to one. Hindus make up about 4 per cent of the population. There are also small Sikh, Jewish, Zoroastrian, and Jain communities.

Singapore's Constitution provides freedom of religion, although the government restricts this right in some circumstances. All religious groups are subject to government scrutiny and must be registered legally under the Societies Act. The government deregistered the Singapore Congregation of Jehovah's Witnesses in 1972 and the Unification Church in 1982, making them unlawful societies. Overall, Singaporeans live in an enviable society where religious harmony and tolerance is such that a Buddhist temple and a Hindu temple can sit side by side on the same street, and have worshippers praying and paying respects not just to either one, but to both.

heritage, housing + landmark projects

There are three facets to Singapore's architecture: it shows the country's multicultural identity and heritage, it addresses the need to provide proper housing for people in an ever-growing city, and it concretises the vision to be at par with the world's great cities.

Thanks to the many different races and religions coexisting here, Singapore is crowded with beautiful buildings such as temples, mosques, churches, and shophouses, whose identities are tied to the people who built, used or lived in them. There are many preserved colonial buildings in the civic district and the race-defined neighbourhoods that Raffles drew up and still exist today. At present, Chinatown, Little India and Arab Street are more tourist destinations than they are homes. Most Singaporeans no longer live in these areas. In fact, they don't live in racially segregated zones anymore. About 90 per cent of Singaporeans live in public housing—government-built, subsidised apartments that dominate the country's suburban landscape.

When Singapore became independent, one of the challenges the government faced was to improve the poor living conditions of most of its new citizens. Thus the first Housing Development Board (HDB) was formed—whose mission was, and still is, to create affordable and attractive housing for the people. Indeed, HDB has been so successful in developing clean and safe public housing for Singaporeans that even some high-income families who can afford private residences live in HDB flats. The Urban Redevelopment Authority (URA) was born in 1974. Its primary task was to develop Singapore's central area and to resettle residents affected by it. In 1989, a new URA was created to become the national planning and conservation authority. Since then, it has been working hard to ensure that the city is able to preserve its past as it develops into the future.

In Singapore, a lot of emphasis is placed on the future. Much of this stems from a Singaporean trait that locals call being "kiasu", or being afraid to lose out. In an age when cities are sometimes ranked by the height of its skyscrapers and the famous names who designed them, it means that Singapore's civic and business leaders—in their quest to put Singapore on the same footing as New York, London or Hong Kong—started as early as the 1980s to commission famous architects like I.M. Pei to build bigger and more elaborate projects here.

THIS PAGE (FROM LEFT): *Designed by I.M. Pei, The Gateway is a striking piece of architecture; multi-coloured spiral staircases of shophouses at Bugis.*

OPPOSITE: *Older flats get a fresh new look, thanks to an upgrading programme.*

Today, downtown Singapore's landscape is as modern as other cosmopolitan capitals in the world. Skyscrapers dot the financial district while grand colonial buildings are preserved and refurbished as hotels or museums.

food: a melting pot

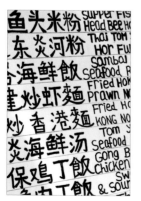

There is perhaps no subject as close to a Singaporean's heart as food. Singaporeans live to eat, and do so well. The country has been described as a culinary goldmine, with a variety of food that is unparalleled in the region. It is in this area that Singapore has perhaps benefited the most from being the region's melting pot. Most famous are the hawkers' varied offerings, which are known simply as hawker food. Grouped in hawker centres, each hawker usually serves only a few specific dishes. Some will serve only one. The range is tremendous; the types of food available are as varied as the different cultures coexisting in Singapore. Some are traditional Indian, Chinese or Malay dishes. Some are fusion dishes whose flavours or use of ingredients are a combination of two or more cuisines. Some favourite hawker dishes include chicken rice, laksa, char kuay teow, yong tau fu, roti prata, satay and nasi lemak.

Singapore is also home to what is known as Nonya cuisine. Also found in Melaka and Penang in Malaysia, this cuisine originated from the Peranakans. The men in this ethnic minority are called Babas, while the women are called Nonyas. Since the cooks in this culture were the women, the resulting Malay-Chinese cuisine was often simply called Nonya food. Nonya food is just one example of the marriage of cuisines that were the product of multiculturalism.

One of Singapore's most famous dishes, fish head curry, is another. This stew, which is unique to Singapore, consists of a large, meaty fish head cooked in Indian curry. It was created by an enterprising Indian restaurateur,

Mr Ayyakkannu of Muthu's Curry. The establishment has won several awards—some from the Singapore Food Festival—and its fish head curry has been widely imitated.

Large Sri Lankan crab fried in a spicy, tomato ketchup-based sauce is another must-try Singaporean dish. Famously known as chilli crab, this is best eaten with the hands. Its thick sauce is so good it is often wiped up with pieces of bread. Many argue about its true origin, but according to Roland Restaurant's owner Roland Lim, chilli crab was created by his mother in the mid-1950s. Today, Roland Restaurant and other equally good seafood restaurants serve chilli crabs daily to tourists and locals alike. Many agree that this is Singapore's best dish.

Restaurants serving cuisine from all over the world can also be easily found. There are French cuisine cooked by chefs trained in three-star kitchens, the best sushi outside of Japan, Royal Thai cuisine, Indian dishes fit for a maharajah, and all-American steaks. In fact, there are few cuisines that are unrepresented in Singapore. Just as diverse as the variety of food on offer are the restaurant designs here: from unpretentious hole-in-the-walls to grand palaces of gastronomy, there is something to satisfy every kind of diner.

THIS PAGE (CLOCKWISE FROM TOP): A wide selection of food at an Indian rojak stall; Hainanese chicken rice, a favourite among locals; chilli crab, another popular dish.
OPPOSITE (FROM TOP): Smith Street at Chinatown comes alive at night when it is closed to traffic and hawkers set up their stalls; a typical Chinese hawker menu.

rest + relax

In Singapore, average temperatures hover between 28°C (82°F) and 32°C (90°F), while the average humidity is 84 per cent. This makes walking a sweaty endeavour. Thus, hanging out in air-conditioned malls—and shopping—is one of Singaporeans' most popular pastimes. On an average weekend, bookstores like Borders or Kinokuniya are packed with people browsing and taking a break from the heat. Movies are also a popular form of recreation, making Singapore one of the countries with the highest per capita cinema attendance.

Meanwhile, the national pastime, eating, has taken on a whole new dimension. With the opening of hip al fresco bars and restaurants at waterfronts, rooftops and shophouses, eating and drinking outdoors has become a trend. Rochester Park, a private enclave along North Buona Vista Road, is fast becoming a very popular place to hang out. Following the successful opening of One Rochester, a charming restaurant nestled amid lush greenery and an exotic landscape, the area is now home to a slew of swanky bars, restaurants and lounges housed in chic, refurbished colonial black and white bungalows built during World War II.

Besides shopping and eating, more Singaporeans are also indulging in outdoor activities such as inline skating, sailing, and scuba diving. The Botanic Gardens has become popular among the young and old for walks and jogs.

uniquely Singapore

In Singapore, the culture, cuisine, arts and architecture of its different peoples blend harmoniously. It is a place where a short walk can lead from seaside to skyscraper, from shophouse to shopping centre, or from conservation area to central business district. Tradition is embraced just as much as modernity, the past is valued as highly as the future. The Singapore Tourism Board's "Uniquely Singapore" campaign promotes Singapore as a city of remarkable contrasts that offers many possibilities, and many places to explore.

THIS PAGE (FROM LEFT): With conservation areas that sit just next to the financial district, Singapore is a place where different elements come together seamlessly; the stylish interior of Grand Hyatt Singapore's StraitsKitchen.

OPPOSITE: One Rochester offers a novel dining experience by combining restaurant service with the cosy setting of a home.

...eating and drinking outdoors has become a trend.

orchardroad

> Esmirada
> Jim Thompson
> Mumbai Sé
> HaKaren Art Gallery
> Mata-Hari Antiques
> Four Seasons Hotel Singapore
> Club 21 Gallery
> Whitebait + Kale

> IndoChine Wisma Atria
> Wisma Atria
> Crystal Jade Jiang Nan Cuisine
> The Link

Istana

> Sheraton Towers Singapore
> Grand Hyatt Singapore
> Singapore Marriott Hotel
> Tangs
> Raoul
> Aliya
> Crystal Jade Golden Palace
> The Carat Club
> Risis

Dunearn Rd
Bukit Timah Rd
Balestier Rd
Stevens Rd
Orange Grove Rd
Nassim Rd
Scotts Rd
Cairnhill Rd
Bukit Timah Rd
Serangoon Rd
Jalan Besar
Cuscaden Rd
Orchard Blvd
Tomlinson Rd
Rochor Canal Rd
Sungei Rd
Ophir Rd
Orchard Link
Orchard Rd
Selegie Rd
Grange Rd
Somerset Rd
Penang Rd
Middle Rd
Rochor Rd
Killiney Rd
Oxley Rd
Victoria St
River Valley Rd
Bras Basah Rd
Stamford Rd
Clemenceau Ave
Alexandra Rd
Singapore River
Esplanade Drive
South Bridge Rd
Pickering St
Cross St

Marina Bay

epicentre of retail therapy

No other street in Singapore is more famous than Orchard Road. What used to be a stretch of dirt road is now a prime shopping area. Once lined with nutmeg plantations, pepper farms and fruit orchards—hence the name—Orchard Road is the city's most densely populated shopping belt today. The 2.5-km (1.6-mile) street cuts across the centre of the city, and some claim it has the largest concentration of shopping malls in the world.

Shopaholics will love the variety of merchandise here. Everything from hard-to-find and outrageously expensive Swiss watches to cheap electronics, the latest European fashion and designer accessories, furniture, gorgeous contemporary artwork and traditional handicrafts, and gourmet food and fine wines can be bought along this consumerist strip. Architecture buffs will admire the designs of the gleaming malls lining both sides of the street, while everyone will just be thankful for the air-conditioning, given the city's hot and humid weather.

Even travellers who are not too fond of shopping will enjoy visiting Orchard Road. The street is home to a vast number of cinemas, restaurants, cafés and bars. Locals and expatriates congregate here to shop, eat and hang out. Walk down Orchard Road on a weekend and you'll feel as if the entire population is there with you. Teenagers hang out at coffee shops, sipping iced mochachinos while furiously sending text messages from the latest hand phones. Foreign workers picnic on the grassy hill at the corner of Scotts Road and Orchard Road. Women in Manolo Blahniks and oversized sunglasses saunter from one designer boutique to another. Muscle men pump iron at the glass-fronted California Fitness Centre. Families walk side by side on every part of the sidewalk, oblivious to the pedestrian traffic jams they're creating. And fighting for space with all these people are booths promoting products and services: credit cards, magazines, holiday packages, canned drinks and hand phones are advertised through loud and crazy road shows, many of which feature or are hosted by local celebrities.

PAGE 30: *One of the most distinctive landmarks along Orchard Road, Singapore Marriot Hotel, reflected on the glass exterior of another icon, Wisma Atria.*

THIS PAGE (FROM TOP): *Stylish additions to the wardrobe from Balenciaga hang in the streamlined store layout; that irresistible four-letter word beckons from a display window.*

OPPOSITE: *During the annual Christmas light-up, Orchard Road becomes ablaze with brilliant lights.*

Orchard Road begins at Tanglin Road and ends at Bras Basah Road. Many tourists are surprised to find that the presidential palace, the Istana, is also located on Orchard Road, its main gate just steps away from the Plaza Singapura Shopping Centre. It is open to the public only on national holidays, and during these public visits, it has become tradition for the President himself to mingle with the people and wish everyone well.

Just off Orchard Road at the historical Emerald Hill is Peranakan Place, a stretch of shophouses built between 1900 and 1930. This group of air-conditioned Peranakan-style shophouses have been turned into several restaurants, pubs and clubs that provide a cosy environment for chilling out. Further up the road are shophouses that have been restored by wealthy owners and converted into homes. This is one of Singapore's most unique residential areas, and a walk here gives a sense of what life must have been like back in the early 20th century.

Orchard Road is a dazzling sight during the holidays, especially during Christmas and Chinese New Year. What started years ago as a simple effort to make Orchard Road more festive has become a massive decorating exercise in which all shopping centres take part. Ornaments hang above the street and adorn the lampposts, and everything is lit with thousands of multicoloured lights. During the Christmas light-up, Orchard Road is transformed into what some liken to Las Vegas. Others dismiss it as kitsch, but year after year, hordes of locals and tourists come to admire it. The first weekend of the Christmas light-up is hell for commuters. Traffic comes to a standstill because of an influx of people driving to the city centre just to see the lights.

In 2005, the Singapore Tourism Board, in partnership with the Urban Redevelopment Authority and other government agencies, launched an Orchard Road redevelopment and rejuvenation initiative. The government is pouring resources and soliciting private investment into remaking Orchard Road so that it has a place among the world's best lifestyle belts and is better than fierce tourism rivals such as Kuala Lumpur, Bangkok, Shanghai and Dubai.

premier shopping belt

Some of the best malls in this shopaholic's mecca include Tanglin Mall, which has become a very popular hangout for expatriate wives who live in the residential areas nearby. Located at the corner of

Tanglin and Grange Roads, it services the needs of the affluent residents in the neighbouring districts. Tanglin Market Place, a gourmet supermarket and bakery and Barang Barang, a home furnishing store, are some of its anchor tenants. The Oaks Grill & Bar is one of the mall's popular dining establishments.

Tanglin Shopping Centre is an old mall known for its Asian antique galleries, tailor shops and stores selling Persian, Pakistani and Afghan carpets. Among the restaurants here is Steeples, a cosy diner that has been serving mouth-watering favourites such as cheeseburgers and peanut butter milkshakes to generations of kids.

Tudor Court is a small row of chic home furnishing shops. Its most notable tenant is Christopher Noto, a young American who runs two shops here: one that carries modern Asian furniture that Noto designs, and another that stocks authentic Asian antiques.

Forum Galleria has a giant toy store and some of the city's best children's boutiques. Clothing and toys of various brands as well as jewellery, electronic goods and men's and women's fashion are also found here.

The marble-fronted Palais Renaissance is the definitive place for upmarket shoppers. Its exclusive boutiques carry international labels such as Prada and DKNY, while posh Indian fashion boutique Mumbai Sé carries contemporary fashion from India's best designers. The Link Home is where chic shoppers pick up homeware, before heading to the Marmalade Pantry for lunch or afternoon tea.

THIS PAGE (FROM TOP): Women on a shopping spree contemplating their next purchase; fitting areas at Tangs are lush and sensual, for the comfort of the modern woman.

OPPOSITE: The conical steel and glass ceiling of Wheelock Place has become a familiar landmark for shoppers.

The Shaw House is always crowded, mostly because of Lido cinema. Its other draw includes the wide range of branded cosmetics at the Isetan department store, and the well-stocked Japanese supermarket in the basement.

Far East Plaza is a teenager's haven: there are over 600 retailers selling mainly hip, edgy street apparel and electronic goods targeted at teens, young adults and the young at heart. There are video stores, electronic shops, cafés, tattoo parlours, and hair and beauty salons, tailors and a number of knick-knack stores. Level One is its most recent development, a basement shopping and lifestyle section located at the mall's basement aimed at attracting even more teens and young adults.

Scotts Shopping Centre's shops count designer boutiques such as Liz Claiborne, Blush and Pois Pois among them that appeal to the modern woman The mall also houses Kiehl's, the highly popular New York pharmacy that sells hair, skin and body care products. Crystal Jade La Mian Xiao Long Bao restaurant, a firm favourite among the locals, and a large air-conditioned food court are found in the basement.

Tangs, the department store connected to the Marriott Hotel, is one of Singapore's oldest stores, having opened in 1932. Owned by the Tang family, it sells everything from household items and apparel to electronics and food. Food lovers flock to the Island Café, which specialises in local hawker food.

The green glass cone-shaped ceiling at the entrance of the trendy Wheelock Place stands out from the line of malls along Orchard Road. It houses the American bookstore chain Borders, the Apple Centre, and a slew of restaurants and fashion boutiques.

Between Ngee Ann City and Orchard MRT station is the bustling passageway to Wisma Atria. This mall has a great range of stores and fashion labels. It is also a chic place to hang out, with flagship tenant IndoChine offering different dining experiences through its al fresco café, oyster bar and beer garden, fine dining restaurant and supper club. Food Republic, its recently refurbished food court, reopened with a nostalgic theme and décor that harkens back to the good old days of scrumptious street fare and tasty treats of the late 20th century, complete with "dim sum" (Cantonese savoury delicacies) pushcarts and traditional Indian and Malay snacks.

Opened in 1994, Ngee Ann City is one of the city's best shopping centres. It offers the best variety of shopping from its anchor tenant, the Japanese department store Takashimaya, the flagship stores of some of the best fashion labels (such as Celine, Loewe, Louis Vuitton, Cartier and Tiffany & Co.), the city's biggest bookstore (Kinokuniya) and a vast array of mid-range trendy boutiques. There are first-rate restaurants on the fourth level and food outlets in the basement level. If you have time for only one mall, this is the one to visit.

Paragon, another of Singapore's best malls, is yet another hot favourite among socialites and women of leisure. Here, high-end fashion reigns supreme with labels such as Prada, Fendi, Gucci, Ftro, Tod's, Valentino and Yves Saint Laurent. Paragon is also home to several classy restaurants such as Lawry's The Prime Ribs, stylish cafés like the PS Café, spa facilities and a well-equipped gym.

Those who seek edgier and funkier street fashion often head to The Heeren Shops. A compact mall comprising a collection of shops with unique product offerings, The Heeren targets shoppers from 24 to 45 years old. With HMV as an anchor tenant, it is known for cutting-edge style and individuality, housing stores that carry cult designer labels and high-end street fashion. Before Level One at Far East Plaza, there was the Annex at The Heeren. Launched five years ago, it was the first specialised section within a shopping mall that is dedicated to teen-oriented stores. Targeting shoppers between 15 to 25 years old, it is still an extremely popular hangout among youth today.

ABOVE: *Malls, including The Heeren Shops, line both sides of Orchard Road.*
OPPOSITE: *Shoppers seeking the perfect fit will be spoilt for choice in Orchard Road.*

Orchard Cineleisure is well-loved for two things: Cathay Cineplex, which has more cinema screens than any other multiplex and some of the best arthouse and independent film selections in town, and iShop, Asia's largest Apple computer store.

Centrepoint is a busy establishment with a good mix of shops offering quality merchandise ranging from books to consumer electronics, and services ranging from laundry to photography. Marks & Spencer, Cold Storage and the local department store, Robinsons, are its anchor tenants. Other than its variety of shops, Centrepoint is also well-known for its flagship store's window displays. The huge shop window for Robinsons stretches along the entire pedestrian street, and over the years it has caught the attention of shoppers and passers-by with its ever-changing fancy window display designs.

After a major facelift, Plaza Singapura has become much better in its mix of retailers, offering everything from teen fashion to furniture. A mall for families and young adults, it has shops for musical instruments, sports equipment, audio and video supplies and household items. Spotlight, one of its flagship tenants, is where homemakers go to buy fabric and other do-it-yourself home furnishing products. Two other hugely popular tenants are the multi-screen cinema Golden Village and the French hypermarket, Carrefour.

THIS PAGE (FROM TOP): Asia's largest Apple computer store, the iShop, is located in Cathay Cineleisure; Orchard Road is a haven for those who seek high-end luxury products.
OPPOSITE: The intersection where some of Orchard Road's most popular malls converge— Scotts Shopping Centre, Shaw House and Tangs.

luxurious accommodations

Despite Singapore's small size, it is home to a vast number of hotels, many of them ranking among the world's best. Most of these larger, well-outfitted hotels are situated near or along Orchard Road, such as Grand Hyatt Singapore, Singapore Marriot Hotel and Four Seasons Hotel Singapore. Besides being famous for their luxurious suites and stellar hospitality, these hotels also attract visitors because of their premier culinary offerings.

mezza9 at the Grand Hyatt Singapore, one of the city's best-known restaurants, has a martini bar that showcases one of the largest selections of martinis in Singapore. Marriot's award-winning Crossroads Cafe is frequented by celebrities and businessmen. Jiang-Nan Chun, the award-winning Cantonese restaurant at the Four Seasons Hotel Singapore, is the venue of choice for countless society dinners and power lunches.

...the city's most densely populated shopping belt...

Four Seasons Hotel Singapore

Nestled in the exclusive tree-lined enclave of Orchard Boulevard, Four Seasons Hotel Singapore is just steps away from the shopping, entertainment and business belt of Orchard Road and a short jog away from the tranquil Botanic Gardens.

The hotel is a convenient 15-minute ride away from Suntec City Convention Centre and the Marina Bay area—an ideal location that allows the perfect mix of business and leisure. The contemporary exterior belies its residential interiors, which are both grand and gracious, evoking a feeling of timeless elegance.

Within is a treasure trove of some 1,500 Asian and international art pieces. Each of the 254 rooms, which includes 40 suites, is designed for maximum comfort, style and efficiency. Great care has been taken to ensure that guests are pampered and their needs well delivered: from custom-designed beds and spacious marble bathrooms, to thoughtful amenities that include DVD/CD players and MP3 cables in all rooms.

For the executive on the go, an exclusive Club Lounge offers a range of benefits at a surcharge. For the health buff,

THIS PAGE (FROM TOP): A refuge deep in the heart of the city; The Living Room's quiet residential interiors evokes a sense of timeless elegance.

OPPOSITE (FROM LEFT): Jiang-Nan Chun is the venue of choice for important gatherings; maximum style and comfort in the Executive Suite.

...its location...makes it an oasis of calm.

a fully equipped 24-hour gym, two swimming pools, two air-conditioned and two outdoor tennis courts and a spa—which offers a comprehensive range of pampering treatments—are available.

Experience exceptional dining at Four Seasons. The culinary fare is a feast for the eyes and the service is impeccable. The contemporary One-Ninety delights with modern international and local cuisine as well as all-time favourites like pasta and pizzas. Its lavish Sunday Champagne Brunch features a selection

of over 50 delectable dishes. A specially set up children's playground provides entertainment for the young ones.

The hotel's award-winning Jiang-Nan Chun is synonymous with style and classic Cantonese cuisine. Its art deco-inspired interiors and discreet service makes it the venue of choice for many society dinners, power lunches and casual family reunions.

Afternoon tea at The Bar at One-Ninety is one of the more pleasurable rituals to be enjoyed after some shopping. Also available are delightful selections

of cocktails and finger food that are perfect for a pre- or post dinner stopover.

Indeed, the legendary service of the Four Seasons is evident in every guest interaction, exemplifying its status as the world's premier operator of luxury hotels and resorts.

The many awards and accolades it has garnered is perfect testament to what the hotel believes in, and guests can always expect the discreet luxury and unsurpassed service which sets it in a class of its own.

FACTS		
ROOMS	254 rooms, including 4 themed suites	
FOOD	One-Ninety: modern European • Jiang-Nan Chun: contemporary Chinese	
DRINK	The Bar at One-Ninety	
FEATURES	collection of Asian and international art • 2 ballrooms • spa • health club • tennis courts • 2 swimming pools • 24-hour room service • car/limousine hire • multilingual concierge staff • high-speed Internet access • business centre • full audio-visual support in function rooms	
NEARBY	Orchard Road • museums • bars and clubs • dining • sightseeing • shopping	
CONTACT	190 Orchard Boulevard, Singapore 248646 • telephone: +65.6734 1110 • facsimile: +65.6733 0682 • website: www.fourseasons.com/singapore	

PHOTOGRAPHS COURTESY OF FOUR SEASONS HOTEL SINGAPORE.

Grand Hyatt Singapore

Grand Hyatt Singapore is not just a hotel. It is an oasis for discerning travellers, allowing them to indulge in every imaginable comfort whilst enjoying the high level of services and outstanding facilities.

Located in the heart of Singapore's premier shopping, entertainment and business district, Grand Hyatt incorporates the principles of Feng Shui in its design. Angled doors at the lobby entrance, a 12-m (40-ft) waterfall and calming water features promote a sense of tranquillity and positive energy.

The Grand Wing, which comprises 399 Grand Deluxe Rooms and suites, boasts luxurious interiors. Keeping in mind the needs of guests who need to be technologically connected, the hotel invested S$1 million to set up an advanced high-speed wired and wireless network so they can access the Internet from anywhere in the hotel, including guestrooms and public areas such as restaurants, the lobby and even the poolside. For in-room entertainment, there are flat screen digital Bang & Olufsen televisions in both the bedroom and lounge area with personal audio video connections. Luxurious goose-down beds and pillows are provided for a restful sleep.

THIS PAGE (FROM TOP): *The amenities in the Grand Room meet the needs of business travellers; subdued hues pervade the spacious Presidential Suite.*

OPPOSITE (FROM LEFT): *The private Grand Club Lounge offers peace and privacy to its guests; the Presidential Suite's living room can be an optional venue for informal meetings; there is a Bang & Olufsen television for personal entertainment.*

The newly refurbished Terrace Wing features Grand Rooms, Grand Club Rooms, a Grand Club Lounge and three Presidential Suites. Warm interiors in a fresh, chic and contemporary design create a relaxed and comfortable ambience that is ideal for both business and leisure travellers.

Guests are surrounded with first class comfort and have access to cutting-edge technology in each of the Terrace Wing's 264 guestrooms and suites. Each guestroom features light-coloured timber interiors and are equipped with spacious workstations that will satisfy the needs of savvy business travellers.

Safes within the rooms are designed to accommodate notebook PCs and other business communication devices. These safes have 24-hour power outlet provisions so laptops can be charged at the same time.

Guests in the Grand Club Rooms and suites have exclusive access to the Grand Club Lounge on the 21st floor, which showcases unsurpassed panoramic views of Singapore's skyline and gardens. Here guests can enjoy complimentary light

refreshments, canapés and evening cocktails as well as continental breakfast. Butler service and private check-in and check-out are also provided.

The business centre provides every convenience for busy executives. And for some much needed downtime, guests can relax at Club Oasis—a total sanctuary of fitness and well-being comprising a spa offering holistic and therapeutic treatments. For those who wish to exercise, there is a fully-equipped gymnasium, golf driving net, aerobics studio and racquet sports facilities which include an indoor badminton hall, two tennis courts and a squash court.

This grand hotel also offers exciting dining options. Its four famed restaurants and three bars provide a full spectrum of innovative dining experiences.

All of these are fast becoming landmark establishments in Singapore's buzzing culinary and nightlife scene.

The sprawling, multi-ethnic mezza9 is justifiably one of Singapore's best-known restaurants. As the name implies, it occupies the mezzanine level of the hotel and derives its name from the nine different dining experiences available.

There is the grill, which offers western grill and rotisserie. Popular dishes include the mixed grill platter with a combination of sirloin steak, char-grilled lamb rack, spiced chicken and handmade sausages. Salmon, lamb and prime rib steaks can be savoured with a wide array of sauces including béarnaise, hollandaise, orange and green peppercorn.

There is a Japanese sushi and sashimi bar, as well as a yakitori grill, with a wide range of fresh seafood, vegetables, meats and condiments.

At the Oriental area which features authentic Chinese cuisine, chefs prepare steamed and wok-fried dishes. Diners can choose from dishes such as steamed garoupa, wok-fried beef and live prawns steamed in lotus leaves.

In addition, there is a European deli and Thai section with appetisers like soft-shell crab and a crustacean bar with fresh seafood that includes oysters, lobster, crab and mussels.

Those with a sweet tooth can indulge themselves in the patisserie. It features classic and contemporary desserts including the cheese platter, a selection of homemade ice creams and the famous Chocolate Fountain only available during the Sunday Brunch.

Rounding out the nine concepts are the walk-in wine cellars and mezza9's martini bar. The restaurant offers a comprehensive selection of white and red wines—as well as champagnes by the glass—to complement food selections, while the martini bar showcases one of the largest selections of martinis in Singapore.

Diners who want to bring the mezza9 experience to their own home kitchens can visit the restaurant's gourmet deli, which stocks chocolates, olive oils, breads, pastries and roasted, grilled and baked items.

The private dining rooms are creatively named washi, teak, obi, silk, cha place, sumi and la cave. Each has its own unique character that is reflected by the furniture, artwork and décor within. Each room can accommodate between eight to 20 guests. mezza9 also offers one of Singapore's most

THIS PAGE (FROM TOP): *mezza9 offers Asian cuisine and a selection of dishes ranging from western grill to seafood; the teak room, one of the private dining rooms; la cave, the wine cellar, is popular for wine tasting sessions.*

OPPOSITE: *There are nine different dining concepts at the mezzanine of the hotel.*

popular Sunday brunches, where guests can enjoy free-flowing champagne.

Wines, champagnes and exquisite gift boxes are available at mezza9. Cakes can be customised for birthdays, office parties and other special occasions. The restaurant's patissiers can help couples design the wedding cake of their dreams.

To experience a uniquely Singaporean showcase of taste, sight and sound, StraitsKitchen is the place to be. StraitsKitchen celebrates the delights of Singapore cuisine in a contemporary market-place setting.

Its remarkable interiors feature warm colours set off by dark timbers, marble and steel. The design features various elements from Singapore's three main cultures— including Chinese teapots, Indian carvings and Malay kampong house wood on the walls. Wood carvings were obtained from local lumberyards and recycled in keeping with the designers' philosophy of incorporating natural elements and materials into the overall design.

Old photographs of Singapore's hawker stalls are displayed on glass partitions, and

THIS PAGE: StraitsKitchen gives a new twist to local cuisine by presenting hawker food in a sophisticated dining environment.

OPPOSITE: Singapore's main ethnic groups are represented in the dishes served at the halal Chinese, Malay and Indian show kitchens.

...the delights of Singapore cuisine in a contemporary market-place setting.

dining areas are accented with wooden sculptures and three-tonne water pumps from supertankers. The furniture is a mix of contemporary pieces and rosewood tables and chairs. It can accommodate 260 diners in various seating arrangements. Couples can cosy up to each other in intimate corners, while larger groups can celebrate special occasions or hold working lunches in semi-private dining areas.

Dining here is a total experience—a multicultural gastronomic tour that is a feast not just for the tastebuds but for all the senses. Forget the usual buffet scenario of food languishing in chafing dishes, wilting in open bowls or drying out under heat lamps.

Diners here get everything fresh and fast. That is because the restaurant's "buffet line" is really a series of show kitchens where chefs take centre stage and all orders are prepared à la minute for the customer. Dishes come straight off the wok, out of the oven, off the grill and onto the plate.

The extensive menu highlights authentic Chinese, Indian and Malay specialties. All the classics of Singapore's culinary tradition are here, such as laksa, mee goreng, fishball noodle soup and Hainanese chicken rice. There is a tandoor oven at the Indian kitchen, and guests can indulge in mouthwatering briyanis, curries accompanied by fresh naan and roti prata. Chefs also

recommend grilled items such as assorted satays, stingray in banana leaf and otak-otak—a quintessentially Singaporean delicacy of minced spiced fish mixed with coconut cream, wrapped in banana leaves and grilled over charcoal.

Another feature of this uniquely Singaporean restaurant is that it is halal-certified. All kitchen procedures and delivery of food and service have been transformed to comply with the requirements of halal certification. The restaurant is often packed at lunch with a mix of foreign and local executives, housewives and tourists.

A newer addition to the hotel's wining and dining options is Oasis, located on the fifth level of the Terrace Wing. This poolside restaurant features a custom-made open charcoal-fired grill where diners can watch their choice of meats and fresh seafood sizzling away while they enjoy drinks. The al fresco setting features tropical foliage and lush greenery, where guests can chill out, unwind and dine in tranquil surroundings—truly an ideal escape from the hustle and bustle of Singapore city life.

Like mezza9 and StraitsKitchen, the restaurant was designed by renowned Japanese interior design firm, Super Potato. The designer wanted to create a contemporary and "healing" space for guests to escape within the city. The ceiling has teak wood panels while walls are adorned with stunning wooden art pieces. Exotic and seasonal fruits are displayed near the bar counter, and polished Thai granite stones accentuate the spacious theatre-kitchen. The all-day dining outlet showcases quick, healthy and simple western and Asian cuisines. There is a range of appetisers, main courses

and desserts to choose from. The sumptuous fare includes all-day breakfast items such as free range scrambled eggs and smoked salmon on brioche, and other mouth-watering selections such as grilled spring chicken with pommery mustard and green salad, a mixed seafood and grilled meat platter for two to share and an array of noodle dishes.

Desserts can be light and refreshing—the chilled honeydew melon with sago and coconut comes to mind—or unapologetically sinful, like the chocolate mud cake. An interesting range of refreshing health drinks—smoothies, shakes, juice blends and a must try homemade lemonade—is also available. The main highlight of the restaurant's culinary offerings is the weekly barbecue buffet dinner and lunch, which feature perfectly grilled meats, sausages and fresh seafood cooked à la minute. The buffets include a free flow of beer, wines and soft drinks. Reservations are highly recommended as the buffets are well-attended.

The 110-seater restaurant features a choice of seating arrangements in a comfortable open setting with ceiling and mist fans. There are intimate corners for up to four persons, as well as a semi-private area at the gazebo for gatherings of up to ten persons. There is also a bar counter that faces the open charcoal-fired grill and an upper deck which can seat up to 35 persons.

The hotel's location in the heart of Orchard Road means world-class shopping for the discerning guests. Retail therapy can begin right at the lobby of the hotel, which houses five specialty boutiques including Roger Dubuis and Bang & Olufsen. High-fashion brands such as Prada and Chanel are only a stone's throw away.

For those who want to experience the lush greenery of the garden city, attractions such as the Botanical Gardens, Jurong Bird Park and Singapore Zoo are all within a 30-minute drive.

THIS PAGE: *After a long day of business or shopping, Oasis is the perfect place to unwind.*

OPPOSITE: *Oasis' outdoor dining area offers a view of the open charcoal-fired grill and poolside.*

FACTS		
ROOMS	663 rooms and suites	
FOOD	mezza9: western, Japanese, Chinese and Thai • Pete's Place: Italian • StraitsKitchen: Malay, Chinese and Indian • Oasis: barbecue	
DRINK	BRIX • Scotts Lounge • martini bar	
FEATURES	business centre • fitness centre • spa • live entertainment	
NEARBY	Orchard Road • shopping • city tours	
CONTACT	10 Scotts Road, Singapore 228211 • telephone: +65.6738 1234 • facsimile: +65.6732 1696 • email: sales.sg@hyattintl.com • website: singapore.grand hyatt com	

PHOTOGRAPHS COURTESY OF GRAND HYATT SINGAPORE.

Sheraton Towers Singapore

Sheraton Towers Singapore has become an icon of impeccable style and service since it first opened its doors in 1985. It is just a 10-minute walk away from the Orchard Road shopping district, with amenities that provide the comfort and convenience that its guests are used to at home. Each of the 413 rooms has a Simmons Beautyrest Systems bed. The hotel uses 100 per cent cotton bed linen and plumed goose down pillows—a tactile treat for the urban warrior.

Rooms and suites are equipped with two-line speaker phones with voicemail system and international direct dialling, flat-screen televisions with teletext, radios, thermostat controlled showers and bedside panels for air-conditioning, lights and alarm clock.

Oriental lampshades and antique Persian rugs are just some of the tasteful furnishings in the deluxe rooms and the hotel's premium accommodations. Sheraton Towers' 23 suites are the jewels in its portfolio. Each have a different theme based on a heritage city. The choice of paintings, furniture, carpets, drapes and other furnishings reflect the distinct character of a particular locale, and celebrate the cultural diversity that continues to fascinate even seasoned travellers.

Deluxe and Royal Suites come with a living room, dining area and pantry, while the Presidential Suite offers state-of-the-art, duplex-style apartment living with all the expected first-class amenities. Guests staying in the suites will enjoy the same benefits as those under the Towers Executive Programme. These include full buffet breakfasts, evening cocktails, hors d'oeuvres and complimentary laundry services.

Sheraton Towers raises the standard of pampering with its fully personalised butler service under the Towers Executive Programme privilege. A morning wake-up call, coffee or tea service, or any other craving—whether it's a local fruit not found on the menu or a sudden desire to fill your room with rose petals—will be attended to by your own butler. With its ability to be attuned to its guests' needs, it's no wonder that the hotel garnered the prestigious Excellent Service award from the Singapore Tourism Board not just once, but several times.

Sheraton Towers also anticipates the needs of the discerning business traveller. Amenities such as plug-and-play high-speed Internet access in all guest rooms, function rooms and the 24-hour business centre make the Sheraton Towers an ideal venue for

THIS PAGE: As in excellent service, the mark of a room's elegance lies in the details. The Edinburgh Suite is a fitting retreat for travellers who consider sleep a luxury.

OPPOSITE: Bringing nature indoors with this garden and waterfall.

business meetings and conferences. Its indoor waterfall and a picturesque garden create an ambience suitable for company retreats.

The grand sweeping staircase that greets guests at the entrance also makes it a popular venue for weddings. A 629-sq m (2,064-sq ft) ballroom is a tasteful blend of Thai, Burmese and Chinese architecture with European stylistic features. No pillars break the view of its broad space, which can seat 550 diners. The 9-colour Axminster carpet and cherry wood panelling give the ballroom the quiet elegance that is characteristic of the hotel. The Lounge in the main lobby plays live music and offers bar snacks such as spicy chicken wings and sugar cane prawns.

Sheraton Towers is well acquainted with the demanding local culinary standards. All three of its restaurants—DOMVS, the Italian Restaurant, Li Bai Cantonese Restaurant and The Dining Room—are award-winning standard bearers of the cuisines they represent, promising a culinary experience worthy of the country's reputation as a food haven. DOMVS, which is Latin for 'home', is an intimate dining restaurant, with an elegant yet comfortable setting that has made it popular with expatriates and locals alike. DOMVS offers unparalleled Italian cuisine and an extensive wine list. A favourite among business travellers is its set lunch, which consists of an appetiser or

THIS PAGE (FROM TOP): *The Rome Suite is decorated with scenes from the ancient civilisation, which includes a painting signed by Uribe; Muted hues of DOMVS, the Italian Restaurant.*

OPPOSITE: *The pond outside is filled with brightly coloured koi.*

soup, a choice from six main courses, two options of desserts and coffee or tea. Li Bai offers the best of Cantonese cuisine in the tradition of the grand Emperors, amidst superb décor and table settings of jade, silver and fine bone. The Dim Sum and Express Business set menus provide selections of Li Bai's signature dishes. Sumptuous choices feature in The Dining Room's buffet menus, combining the best of East and West cuisines.

Food service in every event held at the hotel follows the same culinary standards, regardless of scope or scale. A Meetings and Conference Manager is dedicated to help plan and coordinate functions, attending to details to ensure that events are well-organised and flow smoothly.

The hotel's recreational facilities consist of an outdoor pool, sauna, and a fully-equipped fitness centre. Aerobic classes are available on demand, as are the services of personal physical therapists.

Sheraton Towers' outstanding quality standards, which have set the benchmark in the hotel industry, have earned it a place in the *Condé Nast Traveler* Gold List. *Travel + Leisure Magazine* also voted Sheraton Towers one of the top hotels in the world. Guests experience nothing less than first class service and warm hospitality, making every visit feel like they are coming home to a place where they are treated like family.

FACTS		
ROOMS	413 consisting of 23 suites • 6 cabanas • 384 other types of rooms	
FOOD	Li Bai Cantonese Restaurant: Cantonese • DOMVS, the Italian Restaurant: Italian • The Dining Room: international, Asian and local favourites	
DRINK	The Lounge	
FEATURES	personalised butler service • indoor and outdoor waterfall • open air pool • sauna • laundry and suit press service • gift shop • car/limousine hire	
BUSINESS	high-speed Internet access • 24-hour business centre	
NEARBY	Orchard Road • bars and clubs • dining • sightseeing • city tour	
CONTACT	39 Scotts Road, Singapore 228230 • telephone: +65 6737 6888 • facsimile: +65 6737 1072 • email: sheraton.towers.singapore@sheraton.com • website: www.sheratonsingapore.com	

PHOTOGRAPHS COURTESY OF SHERATON TOWERS SINGAPORE.

Singapore Marriott Hotel

The Singapore Marriott Hotel, situated at the corner of Orchard and Scotts Road, is an instantly recognisable architectural landmark. Its distinctive green-roofed pagoda tower is a beacon of prosperity, an unassuming homage to classical Chinese tradition.

The walkway leads to a lobby that is posh yet understated, a theme that echoes throughout the 30-storey hotel. There are 392 guest rooms and 19 suites, which include the Tang Un Tien Suite and the Pool Terrace Room Collection's Tang Sok Kiar Suite.

The Pool Terrace Room Collection provides a luxurious home in one of Asia's most exciting cities. It comprises ten new rooms which target leisure travellers. Contemporary designs include open concept bathrooms, private verandahs that face the pool and dedicated sunbathing beds. In-room massage therapy options, widescreen flat panel LCD televisions, DVD players and high-speed wireless Internet access are also included in these rooms. From the pool terrace, one can view the modern architecture of adjacent buildings and still enjoy privacy from the bustling street below. The plush 200-sq m (656-sq ft) Tang Sok Kiar Suite has its own private dip pool.

THIS PAGE: A well-appointed room that suits the needs of those who travel on business.

OPPOSITE (FROM TOP): The Singapore Marriott sits in the middle of Orchard Road, right in the centre of the action; The different types of food available at the hotel's several dining locales appeal to a variety of tastes.

Gourmet Summit finalist Chef Irene Soh and the Wan Hao Chinese restaurant, which serves award-winning authentic Cantonese cuisine. Marriott's award-winning Crossroads Cafe is Singapore's premier people-watching nest. It is frequently visited by Singapore's A-list celebrities, artists and business tycoons. Singapore Marriott's prime location, facilities and service make it a premium hotel for the business traveller. Now with an added focus on the leisure traveller, it has also become a top choice for those on urban holiday.

Singapore Marriott has facilities for all guests. It distinguishes itself from the rest with a new outdoor pool boasting a mosaic finish, a jacuzzi and a baby pool. Premium business facilities and services like 24-hour secretarial support ensure that the hotel can double as an office.

The chic, al fresco Pool Grill restaurant serves fresh and contemporary cuisine. The face of the restaurant is Chef Harry Callinan.

He hails from Hunter Valley in New South Wales, Australia and brings 14 years of culinary experience with him. Favourites include the Oriental Seafood Salad with Palm Hearts and Lychee, Classic Bouillabaisse and for those with a sweet tooth, Banana Tart with Butterscotch Sauce.

The Marriott has a host of other dining options: the Marriott Cafe, which has buffet spreads; the Pastry Shop headed by World

FACTS	**ROOMS**	292 deluxe rooms • 72 executive rooms • 17 suites • 9 Pool Terrace Rooms • 1 Tang Un Tien Suite • 1 Tang Sok Kiar Suite
	FOOD	Crossroads Cafe: international and local • Pastry Shop: pastries and light snacks • Marriott Cafe: international buffet • Pool Grill: contemporary • Wan Hao: Cantonese
	DRINK	Bar None: disco • The Living Room: cocktail bar
	FEATURES	limousine service • 24-hour fitness centre • spa • jewellery boutique • tailor • babysitting service • high-speed Internet access • business centre • meeting rooms
	NEARBY	Orchard Road • bars and clubs • dining • sightseeing • city tour • cinema
	CONTACT	320 Orchard Road, Singapore 238865 • telephone: +65.6735 5800 • facsimile: +65.6735 9800 • email: mhrs.sindt.sales@marriotthotels.com • website: www.marriott.com/sindt

PHOTOGRAPHS COURTESY OF SINGAPORE MARRIOTT HOTEL.

Crystal Jade Golden Palace

Mention a high-end Chinese restaurant in Orchard Road that serves mouth-watering Teochew and Cantonese cuisine, and those in the know will have no problem identifying it as Crystal Jade Golden Palace. Strategically located in the midst of Orchard Road, this restaurant is a statement in elegance designed by the well-known SPIN Design Studio of Japan. Its colours, motifs and set-up merge seamlessly into a classy and welcoming ambiance.

Every day, a team of Hong Kong chefs create a spread of top culinary delights for lunch and dinner. Exquisite menu items like Marinated Sliced Goose Meat, Quick-Fried Scallop with Pearl Leaves in Spicy Sauce, Baked Crab in Salted Egg Yolk, and Double-Boiled Soup with Shark's Fin Bone, Bamboo Fungus and Mushroom never fail to elicit the highest compliments from diners.

The restaurant's Teochew cuisine is especially popular, as it uses less oil and has a more delicate taste. The freshest ingredients and the chefs' superb skills have given many discerning diners a reason to make frequent pilgrimages here. Many of the regular gourmets will say that they come for the great food—and that refers to every item on the extensive menu.

At Crystal Jade Golden Palace, things are done a little differently from other Chinese restaurants. Here, they place very

STEAMED LIVE POMFRET IN TEOCHEW STYLE Serves 4

Ingredients

1 pomfret
1 tsp salt
1½ tsp sugar
300 ml (½ pint) chicken broth
2 preserved vegetable leaves
1 tomato, sliced
½ celery stick
3 plums
2 Chinese mushrooms, sliced
1 tsp soya sauce
a thumbsized piece of ginger, sliced thinly
½ chilli

Clean the pomfret and marinate it with salt, sugar and oil. Lay the marinated fish on a plate, and pour chicken broth over it. Spread the rest of the ingredients on the fish. Steam for 20 minutes, and serve.

THIS PAGE (FROM TOP): Personalised service of mouth-watering Chinese dishes; light and healthy Teochew cuisine is popular among the restaurant's patrons.

OPPOSITE: The interiors were done by one of Japan's top designers.

careful attention to food service. While it is a common practice for diners at Chinese-style meals to dip into the dishes, at Crystal Jade Golden Palace, food is first presented on a platter then portioned and served to each diner at the table. The individual portions and attentive personalised service attracts a special clientele—people who are entertaining clients favour this dining locale. Many relationships have been made and various business deals have been sealed in its private VIP rooms.

Readers can bring home a taste of Crystal Jade Golden Palace because the restaurant is sharing the recipe for its top-selling Teochew Style Steamed Pomfret.

FACTS

SEATS	main dining hall: 120 • dining hall: 158 • 2 large VIP rooms: 10–15 diners each • 7 medium VIP rooms: 10–12 diners each • 1 small VIP room: 6–8 diners
FOOD	Teochew and Cantonese • dim sum
DRINK	wine
FEATURES	food is served in individual portions
NEARBY	Orchard Road • Scotts Road • shopping • dining • entertainment • cinema • beauty salons • spas and wellness centres • bookstores • library
CONTACT	290 Orchard Road, #05-22/24 Paragon Shopping Centre, Singapore 238859 • telephone: +65.6734 6866 • facsimile. +65.6736 0020

PHOTOGRAPHS COURTESY OF CRYSTAL JADE GOLDEN PALACE.

Crystal Jade Jiang Nan Cuisine

Crystal Jade Jiang Nan Cuisine presents the finest food from the five provinces of China: Shanghai, Sichuan, Shunde, Huai Yang and Guangdong. The uniqueness of the cuisine lies in its exquisite presentation in vast, enticing varieties.

Designed by the renowned SPIN Design Studio of Japan, Crystal Jade Jiang Nan Cuisine looks nothing like a generic Chinese restaurant. The interiors are done in black and red. There are walls of frosted glass with overlapping floral motifs. Its glass-encased wine cellar is an addition that is also unusual in Chinese restaurants.

Every day, the team of Hong Kong chefs serves an extensive array of culinary masterpieces, Shanghai and Sichuan

delights, together with a selection of superb wines. Set meals and an à la carte menu feature dishes such as crispy Eel in "Wu Xi" Style, Sauteed Fresh Water Shrimp with Salted Egg Yolk, Steamed Pork in Shanghai Style with Bun, Stewed Full Cream Crab Roe with Dried Flour Skin and Sauteed Tianjin Cabbage in Oyster Sauce. A perennial favourite dessert is the sweetened glutinous rice with mixed fruit. Crystal Jade Jiang Nan Cuisine shares the recipe for this dish.

When special occasions call for a get-together, Crystal Jade Jiang Nan Cuisine is the restaurant of choice for many families. It has hosted countless Lunar New Year reunion dinners, where families from different parts of the world come together in an

THIS PAGE (FROM TOP): Savoury dishes served in style; a look that one does not usually find in other Chinese restaurants.

OPPOSITE: Red, which increases the appetite, was a great choice for this dining area.

...an extensive array of culinary masterpieces, Shanghai and Sichuan delights...

SWEETENED GLUTINOUS RICE WITH MIXED FRUIT Serves 1

Ingredients
12 g (½ oz) white glutinous rice
12 g (½ oz) black glutinous rice
2 tsp oil
a pinch of sugar
a pinch of osmanthus
1 tsp raisins
2 dried red cherries
2 red dates
2 lotus seeds

Steam the white and black glutinous rice for 1 hour. Add the oil, sugar, osmanthus and raisins and mix. Lastly, add the dried red cherries, red dates and lotus seeds to the mixture. Stir well. Wrap the mixture in red bean paste. Steam well before serving.

annual gathering to usher in good luck and prosperity for the new year.

Reservations are necessary because the restaurant is always full. Crystal Jade Jiang Nan Cuisine is a restaurant of Crystal Jade Culinary Concepts Holding.

The group, which set up its first Hong Kong-style Cantonese restaurant in 1991, has a reputation for creating fabulous gastronomic experiences, delivering superior service and providing classy but comfortable dining surroundings.

FACTS		
	SEATS	main dining hall: 160 • 3 VIP rooms: 10–15
	FOOD	cuisines from Shanghai, Sichuan, Shunde, Huai Yang and Guangdong
	DRINK	wine cellar
	FEATURES	authentic specialities from the five provinces
	NEARBY	Orchard Road • Scotts Road • shopping • dining • entertainment • cinema • beauty salons • spas and wellness centres • bookstores • library
	CONTACT	391 Orchard Road, #02-12 Ngee Ann City, Takashimaya Shopping Centre, Singapore 238872 • telephone: +65.6238 1011 • facsimile: +65.6733 1011

PHOTOGRAPHS COURTESY OF CRYSTAL JADE JIANG NAN CUISINE.

Esmirada

After making its foray into the Singapore dining scene over a decade ago, Esmirada has since firmly established itself as the "home of authentic Mediterranean cuisine". Colourful and healthy, Mediterranean cuisine depends on the freshness and quality of the ingredients and their careful preparation. The flavours of France, Greece, Italy, Spain and the Middle East are in an array of dishes, which Esmirada serves in generous portions. Paella Española, Italian pasta, juicy meat skewers, spicy Moroccan couscous, Greek moussaka and fresh mussels evoke the riviera's sun-drenched afternoons, quaint town life and its passionate cultures. The spacious surroundings are complemented by dark wood furnishings that are pleasing to the eye and give an elegant yet homely ambience.

Esmirada's restaurants have the key elements to an extraordinary and memorable dining experience. Its good food, extensive selection of wines, superb service, pleasant ambience and lively entertainment will make any gourmand keep coming back for more.

THIS PAGE (FROM LEFT): The Paella Española is great for sharing. Food is served family-style, making Esmirada an ideal place to enjoy a meal with a group; the quality of the ingredients in the salads is evident in the vivid colours and textures; warm lighting and the intimate ambience of all Esmirada restaurants echo even in this open charcoal grill kitchen.

OPPOSITE (FROM LEFT): wine by candlelight adds romance; the restaurant serves delectable freshly grilled seafood and meat skewers.

...waiters perform the zorba, an ancient practice where plates are smashed for good luck.

At Esmirada Orchard, one is immediately transported to the Mediterranean coast. Located next to Orchard Hotel, Esmirada Orchard's rustic elements echo throughout: the interiors are decorated with wrought iron grills and furnished with dark wooden furniture, sofas and bead curtains. For those who prefer al fresco dining, an airy patio with comfortable seats and lush greenery beckons. For an authentic Greek dining experience, waiters perform the zorba, an ancient practice where plates are smashed for good luck.

Separating Esmirada Wine Bar from the restaurant is an impressive walk-through wine cellar. The restaurant, wine cellar and wine bar combined have over 300 wine labels from around the world. Elegant furniture, comfortable sofas and cushions make it a relaxing place to meet for drinks and enjoy good conversation. The wine and cocktail menu is complemented by seasonal tapas.

Esmirada at Chijmes offers a rustic dining atmosphere amid lush greenery, fresh air and romantic candlelight. Enticing aromas waft from the open grill kitchen to three dining areas, two of which are located outdoors. The courtyard has a private section with a garden fountain. The other al fresco dining area has a view of manicured lawns and the 19th-century stained glass windows of the restored Chijmes Hall. The wine cellar stocks a variety of wines that complements Mediterranean cuisine.

FACTS

SEATS	Esmirada at Orchard and Wine Bar: 210 • Esmirada at Chijmes: 160
FOOD	authentic Mediterranean • Mediterranean charcoal grill
DRINK	wine cellar • bar
FEATURES	traditional Greek entertainment • variety of wines
NEARBY	Orchard Road • Raffles City Shopping Centre • Chijmes • Raffles Hotel • Suntec Singapore International Convention & Exhibition Centre • Esplanade – Theatres on the Bay • Marina Square Shopping Centre
CONTACT	Esmirada at Orchard: 422 Orchard Road #01-29 Orchard Hotel, Singapore 238879 • telephone: +65.6735 3476 • Esmirada at Chijmes: 30 Victoria Street, #01-17 Chijmes, Singapore 187996 • telephone: +65.6336 3684 • email: orchard@esmirada.com, chijmes@esmirada.com • website: www.esmirada.com

IndoChine Wisma Atria

Dominating a prime corner of Orchard Road is IndoChine Wisma Atria, a stylish complex consisting of dining and drinking establishments. It opened its doors in September 2004 and has since become an entertainment institution among shoppers and partygoers.

Nude + Supperclub offers flavoursome Indochinese cuisine. Greenery provides cool shade while a water wall separates

*THIS PAGE (FROM TOP): **The sumptuous seafood platter is a favourite amongst IndoChine regulars; casual dining at the stylish Nude + Supperclub.***

OPPOSITE (FROM LEFT): Delectable seafood dishes adorn the Indochinese menu; enjoy cocktails and wine at Sanctuary Garden.

restaurant patrons from the street crowd. Dining at Nude + Supperclub is a gastronomic adventure that is easy both on the wallet and the waistline. The extensive menu of traditional Cambodian, Vietnamese, and Laotian dishes includes Pho Bo (beef noodle soup), Bun Tom Nuong (rice vermicelli with grilled prawns) and other healthy but equally mouth-watering alternatives.

Adjacent to Nude + Supperclub is Sanctuary Garden, which has revolutionised

the nightclub scene. Enjoy performances from live bands in the evening and during the day, beer, snacks and live sports screenings make Sanctuary Garden an ideal place for men to hang out while the women go shopping.

FACTS		
	SEATS	Nude + Supperclub: 50 • Sanctuary Garden: 100
	FOOD	contemporary Indochinese
	DRINK	Old and New World wines • cocktails
	FEATURES	café • wine cellar • bar • resident bands
	NEARBY	Orchard Road • Takashimaya Shopping Centre • Shaw Centre
	CONTACT	435 Orchard Road, Wisma Atria, Singapore 238877 • telephone: +65.6333 5003 (Nude + Supperclub), +65.6238 3473 (Sanctuary Garden) • facsimile: +65.6734 1241 • email: enquiry@indochine.com.sg • website: www.indochine.com.sg/wisma.htm

Whitebait + Kale

stone's throw away from Orchard Road is Whitebait & Kale, a casual yet stylish dining destination. Complemented by a deli, wine shop and bar, the restaurant is a gem tucked away at the iconic Camden Centre, which is easily accessible from the shopping district yet offers solace from the hustle and bustle of the city.

Spread over more than 280 sq m (3,000 sq ft), Whitebait & Kale offers a contemporary indoor dining space, coupled with a breezy al fresco section. The atmosphere is truly inviting and intimate—akin to a summer beach house, dotted with warm wooden benches and lazy Adironack chairs on the outside. Inside, cool marble tabletops, nautical-blue fabrics with white piping and whitewashed floorboards create a laid-back setting that is effortlessly chic and welcoming. Inspired by Mediterranean, European and Australian

cuisine, the feel-good comfort food here showcases a range of wholesome flavours and fresh seasonal ingredients.

The ever-changing menu is a constant delight for customers who welcome new tastes and intriguing creations during their regular promotions. Emu, paper bark and mountain pepper are just some of the exotic ingredients that have made their way from the kitchen to the dining table.

Guests can also look forward to signature dishes like its Lobster Bisque with tarragon oil, Baked Snapper Pie and Beer-battered Fish & Chips—guaranteed to make them come back for more. Those with bigger appetites will relish the generous cuts of free range meats and hearty servings of wholesome pasta and gourmet salads (Roasted Pumpkin with Endive, Marsala Prunes, Pistachio and Feta Cheese, anyone?).

THIS PAGE: Old favourites get a new twist from the creative chef.

OPPOSITE: Whitebait & Kale has ample space for parties and big corporate functions.

Do leave room for the decadent homemade desserts, from an exquisite Pavlova to a rich Valrhona Chocolate Savarin with Grand Marnier orange sauce. The restaurant serves lunch from 12.00 pm to 2.15pm, and dinner from 7.00pm to 10.00 pm from Monday to Saturday.

Aside from the à la carte menu, there are also gourmet set menus for lunch and dinner, topped with daily blackboard specials featuring the fresh catch of the day and seasonal finds. At the popular Sunday brunch from 10.00 am to 4.00 pm, guests can tuck into their favourite breakfast items including Eggs Benedict with dill mustard sauce, fluffy Belgium Waffles and Ricotta Pancakes, all washed down with a choice of quality bubbly from the award-winning wine list.

With over 150 labels to choose from, Whitebait & Kale's wine selection offers something for everyone and covers a wide spectrum of wines across different countries, regions and varietals. Particularly impressive are some rare boutique wines sourced and imported directly from producers in Australia and New Zealand. What's more, there are 21 different wines served by the glass, allowing guests to experiment with new labels to match their meal. Do look out for the Pick of the Month, which puts unique boutique wines in the spotlight. All the wines are available at the restaurant, bar and wine shop, so you can even take away a ready-chilled bottle to enjoy.

Whitebait & Kale also features a bar, equipped with a cosy lounge and porch where guests can sip one-of-a-kind concoctions such as its popular Espresso Martini—a blend of Smirnoff vodka, De Kuyper Butterscotch Schnapps and coffee beans. Apart from the classic freshly muddled Mojito, you can also request for it to be blended into a smooth mix of Cachaca rum, lime juice, mint syrup and mint leaves. Other delicious options presented on the carte are Whitebait & Kale's Signature Martini—containing

Tanqueray gin, pineapple and lime juice and Charleston Aruba with a lemon twist; and Whitebait & Kale Breezer, combining Absolut Vanilla, Blue Curacao, pineapple juice, apple juice and Sprite. The bar is open from 6.30 pm to 12.00 am from Monday to Saturday.

The self-service deli serves breakfast and bites for a quick lunch on the go or a leisurely teatime. Dine in or take away a range of irresistible items such as homemade cakes, desserts, muffins and scones. The gourmet sandwiches, featuring either ciabatta or wholemeal bread, come with chips and salads. Hot Corned Beef with Swiss Cheese and Sauerkraut, Smoked Norwegian Salmon with Cream Cheese and Capers, and Grilled Veggies with Hummus Spread are only some of the delicious combinations found at the deli. Also available are freshly blended fruit juices, milkshakes made from New Zealand's Kapiti gourmet ice cream, Numi organic teas and coffee drinks that use Whitebait & Kale's house blends. The deli is open from 8.30 am to 5.00 pm every day except Sunday.

Another highlight at Whitebait & Kale is the Chef's Table carved from the wine shop space that is reserved for private dining. The large oakwood communal table seats 10, and guests can choose from a

...a casual dining experience with a very personal touch...

variety of Chef's Table personalised menus. Opt for a degustation of the restaurant's most popular dishes. Alternatively, a "home-style service" menu can be created to suit your personal tastes and preferences. It would be like having a private home party with every whim and fancy catered for. Offering a casual dining experience with a very personal touch is something Whitebait & Kale is proud of.

Whitebait & Kale is a popular venue for dinner parties, product launches and other corporate events. The indoor dining area, al fresco section and bar can be booked separately, or as a single venue for grander functions. Finger food menus, set menus and beverage packages can be customised to accommodate specific needs. It is no wonder people keep coming back for more.

FACTS		
SEATS	130 • main floor: 60, Chef's Table: 10, bar: 26, al fresco: 47
FOOD	contemporary western
DRINK	boutique wines • over 150 labels
FEATURES	personalised menus at Chef's Table • daily blackboard specials • set gourmet menus
NEARBY	Orchard Road • Tanglin Mall • Tanglin Shopping Centre • Singapore Visitors Centre • Singapore Tourism Board • Botanic Gardens • city tours
CONTACT	1 Orchard Boulevard, Camden Centre #01-01, Singapore 248649 • telephone: +65.6333 8697 • facsimile: +65.6333 8035 • email: marcom@whitebaitandkale.com • website: www.whitebaitandkale.com

Aliya

A specialty jewellery, fashion and home décor store, Aliya is the brainchild of Bianca Pereira, a self-taught designer and an expert in semi-precious stones.

Guided by her knack for choosing beautiful stones and decorative items, Pereira has, in the span of seven years, transformed Aliya into one of Singapore's respected jewellery brands. What began as a tiny kiosk in Suntec City soon became part of Singapore's burgeoning jewellery retail industry. Aliya now has two outlets: one in Paragon Shopping Centre and another in Raffles City Shopping Centre.

A trip to India was what first sparked the idea for Aliya. Pereira was living in Sri Lanka at the time. She conceived Aliya, which is Singhalese for elephant, as a brand that would celebrate each person's unique characteristics. It is therefore a departure from the look of branded fashion accessories. Instead, it offers an individualistic approach to jewellery.

The store carries around 50 different stones of various shapes and sizes in unique settings. Stones like agate, garnet, amethyst, aquamarine, prehnite, peridot, chrysoprase, black star, diopside, jasper

THIS PAGE: *Jewellery and fashion accessories share store space with home décor.*
OPPOSITE: *The range of products shows the ingenuity and creativity of Aliya's owner.*

...an individualistic approach to jewellery.

and sandstone come from as far as Brazil and Africa. Pereira buys the stones from a dealer and then works with her gifted silversmith in Jaipur, India, an area renowned for its master craftsmen.

Some of Aliya's pieces are Pereira's own creations, which she designs in Singapore then sends to Jaipur for production. Most of Aliya's rings are

stones set in silver and cost an average of S$120. Some pieces are one-off items, while other have designs that use calibrated stones, which allow reproductions to be made. Apart from the sterling silver jewellery that Aliya is well-known for, the store also carries a collection of fashion jewellery that includes crystal and Murano glass pendants.

...an eclectic mix of jewellery, fabric, home furnishings, accessories and gifts.

Some of the more unique items on display include an abaca-banana fibre screen that can also be used as a picture holder; a black Kukui nut necklace that demonstrates Pereira's affinity for organic materials; an immaculately finished ebony and shagreen (stingray skin) bracelet; and rutilated quartz crystals from Brazil.

Aliya caters to customers with a daring sense of style. Those who want their outfits to make a statement will find a lot of choices among the array of eye-catching jewellery and accessories. Aliya's bold designs convey fashion confidence, and Pereira expertly treads the narrow line between the adventurous and the outrageous.

THIS PAGE (FROM LEFT): This ornament pays tribute to the magnificent animal that is the inspiration for the store's name; treasures can be found in every nook and cranny.

OPPOSITE: Gift items amd home accessories come in varied styles to suit different tastes.

The store in Paragon is filled with an eclectic mix of jewellery, fabric, home furnishings, accessories and gifts. Visiting the outlet in Paragon is like entering a giant treasure trove, which Pereira is wont to liken to Ali Baba's cave.

The store in Raffles City, which is frequented by working professionals, has a streamlined display of Aliya's more modern collections. The relaxed, bohemian feel of this outlet allows customers to pore over her trademark sterling silver jewellery, semi-precious stones, glittery bangles, Indian cotton shawls, paper vases, and necklaces.

Aliya's jewellery has appeared in fashion magazines such as *Nuyou*, *Her World* and *Style Magazine*.

Pereira's fashion adage, 'good line and good form are timeless' guides her business as it adapts to changing trends and the shifting demand from big brand to individually designed jewellery.

FACTS

PRODUCTS	jewellery • fashion accessories • home furnishings • lamps
NEARBY	shopping • Orchard MRT station • dining • Esplanade – Theatres on the Bay
FEATURES	jewellery advice
CONTACT	290 Orchard Road, #03-47 The Paragon, Singapore 238859 • 252 North Bridge Road, #02-21 Raffles City Shopping Centre, Singapore 179103 • telephone: +65.6836 1403 (The Paragon), +65. 6339 3186 (Raffles City) • email: aliya@pacific.net.sg • website: www.aliyastore.com

The Carat Club

The Carat Club is located in the charming Emerald Hill area just a stone's throw away from the the premier Orchard Road shopping belt. Customers can browse through the boutique's comprehensive selection of jewellery-related publications or sip tea while being attended to by highly-trained personal jewellers.

The boutique's signature product is the Love Diamond, a 58-facet hand-cut stone that reveals eight perfect hearts and eight perfect arrows when seen under a loupe. Set in white gold, it comes in two cuts—round brilliant and square—that show off its perfect symmetry and excellent polish. The Carat Club is known for its diamonds particularly among those who require large carats. Clients with specific requirements will find stones of every cut, colour and clarity here.

Everyday Treasures, another line, offers reasonably-priced diamond pendants and rings that have become a hit with young women. Popular pieces from this collection include alphabet charms, which can be hung from a bracelet or used to spell out one's initials on a chain.

Apart from its own special creations, The Carat Club also carries world-renowned foreign collections. Florentine brand La Nouvelle Bague pairs diamonds with

THIS PAGE (FROM TOP): Coloured and clear diamonds are fashioned into elegant works of art; an inviting retreat where customers could feel at ease while learning the finer points of jewellery appreciation.

OPPOSITE (FROM TOP): Eye-catching tattoo-inspired collection from Stefan Hafner; bracelet from La Nouvelle Bague's Foglie oro Giallo line.

the company to offer a range of superbly crafted, trend-setting jewellery collections.

Financial analyst Chan Boon Yong, who comes from a family that manages a leading diamond wholesaler in the region, dreamt of starting his own luxury jewellery boutique.

In 1997, he set up The Carat Club in an elegant bungalow in Bangsar, Kuala Lumpur. The company has since opened three more branches in Kuala Lumpur and one branch in Singapore.

enamel. Pieces from Stefan Hafner's line of award-winning diamond jewellery are available, as well as jewelled watches from the Leon Hatot collection. These design-intensive watches feature bezels set with diamonds and other precious stones.

Although diamonds are The Carat Club's forte, it also carries coloured gemstone and pearl jewellery. It offers jewellery cleaning and preservation services, as well as a custom jewellery design service for clients who need something for a special occasion, or simply want something unique for themselves.

The Carat Club's fine-jewellery manufacturing arm fuses Italian design, Malaysian craftsmanship and German technology. This in-house capability allows

FACTS

PRODUCTS	Diamond, gemstone and pearl jewellery
FEATURES	custom jewellery design • jewellery appreciation talks and publications • jewellery cleaning and preservation services
NEARBY	shopping • dining • sightseeing • city tours • cinemas
CONTACT	15 Emerald Hill Road, Singapore 229297 • telephone: +65.6738 1368 • facsimile: +65.6235 1389 • email: tccspore@thecaratclub.com • website: www.thecaratclub.com

PHOTOGRAPHS COURTESY OF THE CARAT CLUB.

Club 21 Gallery

Exquisite, artistic, stunning—every item in Club 21 Gallery is an art piece truly befitting its place in this showroom. Located at Four Seasons Hotel, the gallery is adjacent to the Club 21 boutiques, a collection of exclusive high-fashion retail outlets. In a similar vein, the gallery is conceptualised to complement the boutiques with its collection of exquisite home accessories and decorations.

Every item available in this gallery is one-of-a-kind, so there are plenty reasons for weekly visits to check out the new arrivals.

Here, you'll find elegant wine glasses, goblets and vases made from Murano glass. The artisans from the Venetian island of Murano produced these stunning pieces using techniques that date back more than seven centuries. Their skill and craftsmanship are renowned internationally, as they make glassware with age-old methods like millefiori (using multi-coloured glass) and aventurine (gold thread) techniques.

The gallery also offers glassware by Anna Torf from Poland. Each design is distinctive in both form and function. From whimsical to conventional shapes, single colours to bold splashes, delicate transparency to dark opaque, each design naturally becomes a conversation piece.

These elegant vases are art pieces in themselves, but for those who are reluctant to

Every item available in this Gallery is one-of-a-kind...

and beautiful candlebras, such as the ones by Italian Vanin Giancarlo and French Les Heritiers, can be found here.

At the gallery, one can literally get all the best quality designer wares from all over the world to jazz up the home. From platinum-glazed porcelain crockery to cutlery featuring buffalo-horn handles, one can also find lovely hand-embroidered table runners, cushion covers and bed linens.

Great designs from Asia are also readily available. From Vietnam, Collection Indochine's tall lacquer vases are recent additions that quickly gained a loyal following. Using no fewer than 23 layers of lacquer, the vases' radiant, gleaming lustre is simultaneously bold yet soothingly subtle.

Eclectic collections are elegantly displayed with a fine attention to detail at Club 21 Gallery. The showroom presents the best designer homeware and home accessories from all over the world in a refined and distinctive space.

leave something so beautiful as an empty display object will be pleased to know that the gallery often organises floral workshops for happy owners to fully appreciate the innumerable ways that they can showcase and enjoy their fabulous purchases.

Candelabras are a must-have in many luxury homes and Club 21 Gallery features a marvellous collection to choose from. Modern and inspired designs from renowned artists will complement any home décor,

THIS PAGE (FROM TOP): Exquisite glassware from Anna Torf are great display pieces that will brighten up any home; Peter Bruers's arresting black and white vases and plates are all individually crafted and hand painted.

OPPOSITE: The gallery has an ever-changing window display, enticing shoppers to visit often.

PHOTOGRAPHS COURTESY OF CLUB 21 GALLERY.

FACTS

PRODUCTS glassware • stoneware • lacquerware • artworks • tableware • table linen • bedding • cushion covers • lamps • home accessories • French tea

FEATURES shipping services • floral workshops

NEARBY Orchard Road • Scotts Road • shopping • dining • city tours

CONTACT 190 Orchard Boulevard #01-07/8, Four Seasons Hotel, Singapore 248646 • telephone: +65.6887 5451 • facsimile: +65.6735 2993 • website: www.clubtwentyone.com

HaKaren Art Gallery

Near the Orchard Road shopping belt is an art gallery well-known among international art connoisseurs for its contemporary Chinese art. HaKaren Art Gallery brings the work of outstanding Asian artists to a global audience, with its collections of paintings and sculptures from some of China's best contemporary artists. HaKaren's name in Mandarin combines three words: 'Ke', which means guest, 'Yi', which means artist and 'lang', which means gallery—befitting a venue that brings guests and artists together in a cross-cultural exchange.

Founder and director Derek Tse is a professional graphic designer and illustrator by training. HaKaren is the result of his love for China and its art, history

...a venue that brings guests and artists together in a cross-cultural exchange.

HaKaren has held more than 100 exhibitions and art events all over the world. Some of the art pieces in its collection have been entered in premier auctions in Asia, proof of the high standard of its paintings. Multinational corporations and international banks are among HaKaren's esteemed clients, as are financiers, academic professors and influential members of the cultural community. Apart from catering to its clients' sophisticated tastes, the gallery also offers art investment consultations.

HaKaren increases knowledge and helps deepen the understanding of China's proud heritage through the catalogues it produces and the events it organises. It hosts artist demonstrations and performances both in Singapore and abroad, including the renowned China National Museum of Fine Art in Beijing and New York City. HaKaren hosts charity events as well, where profits from selected shows are donated to aid organisations.

and culture. Perhaps this stemmed from being the first foreign student to enter the country during the early 1980s, or from a more deep-seated affiliation prompted by his Chinese roots. Whatever the reasons, he regards the works of the gallery's artists with affection and appreciation, and he made HaKaren a vehicle for educating and broadening the public's interest in them.

FACTS

PRODUCTS contemporary oriental paintings • sculptures • prints • catalogues

FEATURES exhibitions and art fairs • demonstrations and performances • portrait commissions • art investment consultation

NEARBY Orchard Road • Scotts Road • shopping • city tours

CONTACT 19 Tanglin Road, #02-43 Tanglin Shopping Centre, Singapore 247909 • telephone: +65.6733 3382 • facsimile: +65.6735 9709 • email: enquiries@hakaren.com • website: www.hakaren.com

PHOTOGRAPHS COURTESY OF HAKAREN ART GALLERY.

Jim Thompson

the company he founded is still going strong, with a wide product range and a presence in numerous countries in Asia and elsewhere. In Singapore, there are five Jim Thompson outlets offering an array of Thai silk products from home furnishings and accessories to fashion and gift items.

For the home, there are silk cushions—plain, printed or textured, all in vibrant colours. Coordinated place mat and napkin sets are also available.

The company has also branched out into furniture, producing distinctive, East-meets-West collections that highlight contemporary Thai design. Pieces include daybeds, sofas, occasional and bedside tables crafted from solid timbers and exquisite fabrics. Gifts and accessories include purses, picture frames, cigarette

THIS PAGE: *It is difficult to discuss Thai silk without mentioning Jim Thompson. The company he founded has expanded its product range beyond textile and fashion to include items from furniture to food.*

OPPOSITE: *An array of silk and cotton fabrics that come in plain colours as well as with Jim Thompson's signature print designs.*

Convinced that Thai silk could capture the imagination and interest of overseas buyers, American James Thompson established the Thai Silk Company after the Second World War. He and his company are widely credited for reviving Thailand's dying silk industry and bringing its products to the attention of the world.

In 1967, Jim Thompson mysteriously disappeared in Malaysia's Cameron Highlands. By then however, the industry had grown by leaps and bounds. Today,

...Thai silk products from home furnishings and accessories to fashion and gift items.

and spectacle cases, wine sacks, tissue holders, vanity kits and jewellery boxes.

For children or the young-at-heart, there are adorable teddy bears and elephants made from silk, cotton and chenille. The emphasis of course is on the lustrous, shimmering fabric that is also most evident in the variety of fashion items on offer.

Women can choose from a ready-to-wear collection of plain or printed silk blouses, skirts and scarves, while for men there are shirts and neckties. Formal or informal, plain or flamboyant, the products incorporate uniquely Thai elements into contemporary designs.

The company produced a line of fashionable handbags and beach bags that use the finest leathers—cowhides from Spain, lambskin and goatskins from Southern France—in combination with the company's own home furnishing fabrics. The beach bags are made from light or heavy canvas decorated with various Jim Thompson signature prints.

Customers can also purchase plain or printed silk and cotton fabrics for clothing as well as for upholstery.

Jim Thompson also has outlets in neighbouring Malaysia. Apart from carrying Thai silk products, one of its outlets serves authentic Thai cuisine: Mythai restaurant is located at Starhill Gallery in Kuala Lumpur. They will open another restaurant in Pangkor Laut island in late October 2006.

PHOTOGRAPHS COURTESY OF JIM THOMPSON.

FACTS

PRODUCTS	Thai silk • clothing • gifts and accessories • home furnishings
FEATURES	contemporary Thai furniture
NEARBY	shopping • dining • sightseeing • city tours • cinemas
CONTACT	Palais Renaissance: 390 Orchard Road #01-08 & #02-10, Singapore 238871 • Takashimaya: 391 Orchard Road, Ngee Ann City B1, Singapore 238873 • DFS Scottswalk Level 1: 25 Scotts Road, Singapore 228220 • Raffles Hotel Arcade: 1 Beach Road #01-07, Singapore 189673 • telephone: +65.6323 4800 • email: siamsilk@singnet.com.sg

The Link

THIS PAGE (FROM TOP): *The Link bagbar, The Link Wedding, alldressedup and The Link.*

OPPOSITE (CLOCKWISE FROM LEFT): *Etro, Miss Sixty, Energie and The Link Home.*

The Link is an established fashion and lifestyle boutique that features designer labels. Founded by Tina Tan-Leo over 20 years ago, The Link Group opened the first Gianni Versace store outside of Italy in 1979. As a pioneer of the multi-brand acquisition concept, The Link has the ability to spot and set trends and has introduced many international labels to Singapore and the region. At a time when designer labels were still relatively new in Asia, it was The Link's vision of setting the standard for high-end retail in Singapore that forged these ventures. The group is now aiming to set up concept stores in the region and to expand its name to the global arena. The Link umbrella includes personal shopping, interior styling services, bridal gift registry, corporate gift and hamper services, giving its sophisticated customers a truly integrated shopping experience.

Monobrand stores under The Link Group include Etro, Miss Sixty and Energie. Boutiques carrying these labels can be found at Paragon and The Heeren Shops along Orchard Road. Italian fashion label Etro is famous for its scarves, bags and fragrances, with an elegant style that appeals to both men and women. Miss Sixty's collection of clothing from the 1960s to the 1980s caters to young women. Its male counterpart, Energie, caters to young men who have the eye for urban styles and innovative design. Women can find apparel to match their individual style at alldressedup in Mandarin Gallery. For those who are keen on global fashion trends, The Link in the same shopping gallery lines up the best

of the international labels like Alberta Ferretti, Chloe and Roberto Cavalli.

The Link bagbar at Paragon presents a new store concept—clients sit at the bar where bags are served on suede platters. There is a showcase of vintage collectibles and an exclusive designer collection from big names such as Judith Leiber, Renaud Pellegrino and Rodo.

Bridal and evening wear are available at The Link Wedding, which also includes Vera Wang and Reem Acra Bridal.

The Link Home at Palais Renaissance offers the best in home living, with the finest linen, silk cushions, silver, glassware, stemware and bed and bath accessories. It also carries The Link's own product lines for beauty and bath, and fragrances.

FACTS

PRODUCTS men's and women's fashion • accessories • bridal • homeware and furnishings

FEATURES personal shopping • interior styling services • bridal gift registry • corporate gift and hamper services

CONTACT The Link/alldressedup, #02-01/01-01 Meritus Mandarin, 333 Orchard Road, Singapore 238867 • The Link Home, #01-10 Palais Renaissance, 390 Orchard Road, Singapore 238871 • The Link Wedding, Level 1 Shangri-la, Orange Grove Road, Singapore 258350 • The Link bagbar/Etro/Miss Sixty, #01-31/01-30/02-29 Paragon, 290 Orchard Road, Singapore 238859 • Energie, #02-01 The Heeren Shops, 260 Orchard Road, Singapore 238855 • Miss Sixty #02-47/47A Wisma Atria 435 Orchard Road, Singapore 238877 • press office: telephone: +65.6736 0645 • facsimile: +65.6733 7251 • website: www.thelink.com.sg

PHOTOGRAPHS COURTESY OF THE LINK.

Mata-Hari Antiques

world. A number have even found places in museums and private collections. Mata-Hari, however, is by no means highbrow. In fact, its owner hopes to make art more accessible to the masses.

In the display windows are silk slippers and caps from China, intricately woven ethnic jackets and wooden statues from Papua New Guinea. Look closely and you'll see a bottomless canoe from Papua New Guinea leaning against one corner. This extraordinary piece, which has beautiful carvings of animals and is festooned with cassowary feathers, is used in initiation rites for boys.

The shop has an impressive array of Asian treasures hung on its walls and laid out in glass cases and wooden shelves.

Tucked away in a quiet corner of Tanglin Shopping Centre is Mata-Hari Antiques, a treasure trove of rare Asian art and antiques. Opened 18 years ago by Genevieve de Bernis, it is the realisation of a lifelong passion for art and art history.

When Genevieve arrived in Singapore in 1984, she fell in love with Asian art. Three years later, she opened Mata-Hari. She travels regularly, combing Asia for extraordinary finds. Many pieces from her shop have since found homes around the

THIS PAGE: Exquisite pieces that reveal remarkable skills in sculpture, metalwork and jewellery making.

OPPOSITE: Treasures that speak of the customs and traditions of cultures long forgotten.

...a treasure trove of rare Asian art and antiques.

There are intricate silver trinket boxes from Cambodia, ornate gold jewellery from Asian nations, delicate silk textiles from Bhutan, and antique lacquerware from Indochina.

Ethnic beaded jewellery from northern India are displayed beside antique batiks and kebayas from the Peranakan, while beautiful Tibetan amulets and bowls made from silver, turquoise and jade are arranged in a glass cabinet. Antiques, however, are not the only things one will find in this shop. Silver and gold jewellery are reset and remodelled to suit modern tastes. Antique crystal amulet pendants from Cambodia and Tibetan coral and sea beads have been remounted in gold. Semi-precious stones on antique gold jewellery give these heirloom pieces a new twist. Many items are rare, like the Burmese opium weights that are decorated with detailed carvings of animals, some of which are only the size of a small thumbnail. The silk textiles from Bhutan are also hard-to-find, as are the Indonesian gold betel nut cutters that are moulded into intricate animal shapes such as the legendary garuda.

Other gems are old bronze temple bells and ceremonial candleholders from Cambodia called popil—Mata-Hari is the only shop in Singapore that carries them.

Visiting Mata-Hari is truly like taking an overview of Asian art history—the objects within speak of the region's rich culture and traditions.

FACTS		
PRODUCTS	Asian antiques • jewellery • Asian art • batik • clothing • lacquerware • homeware
FEATURES	rare and hard-to-find Asian art and artefacts
NEARBY	Orchard Road • Tanglin Mall • Tudor Court • Scotts Road • shopping • dining
CONTACT	19 Tanglin Road, #02-26 Tanglin Shopping Centre, Singapore 247909 • telephone: +65.6737 6068 • facsimile: +65.6738 3579 • email: bernis@singnet.com.sg

Mumbai Sé

Located in Palais Rennaissance along Orchard Road is the fashion and lifestyle boutique, Mumbai Sé. Meaning 'from Mumbai' in Hindi, Mumbai Sé adds a touch of Bollywood to the shopping scene in Singapore. Limestone walls and walnut panels provide an elegant background to the 464 sq m (5,000 sq ft) of space, which showcases high-end contemporary Indian fashion, jewellery and accessories from the hottest designers in India.

India's romance and mysticism are captured in prêt-à-porter outfits, evening wear and elaborate dresses with Swarovski crystals, intricate embroidery and beadwork. The collection from Ashish N Soni reflects classic simplicity. Creations from Satya Paul, whose women's wear line has won international accolades, gives Indian style a cosmopolitan look. The outifts by Rocky S are as young and trendy as the costumes he designs for Bollywood films.

Ranna Gill, Renu Tandon, Shantanu & Nikhil, Geisha, Monisha Jaising, Isha and Mana Shetty complete the impressive roster of designers represented here. Their designs are worn not only by top Bollywood stars but by Hollywood celebrities as well. Even

acclaimed directors like Luc Besson have featured some of these designers' creations in blockbuster films such as Moulin Rouge. All designers featured in the shop are making their mark in America and in Europe's fashion capitals.

Mumbai Sé's collection of bold, colourful jewellery uses precious and semi-precious stones. Rose-cut diamonds, tourmaline and South Sea pearls are transformed into pieces that complement contemporary Indian fashion.

A quarter of the store is devoted to home furnishings, décor and artwork. Luxurious but affordable furnishings include lounges, stylish couches and armchairs made with sterling silver. Home décor is comprised of sterling silver tea sets and silver vases with rosewood bases. Pieces from Ravissant, India's first designer label, figure prominently here. Master craftsmen are responsible for Mumbai Sé's collection of artwork, which is comprised of

rose-themed and Buddha-inspired paintings, contemporary crystal Ganesha figurines and modern interpretations of the Buddha.

At Mumbai Sé, the essence of India is combined with contemporary designs from the west, and the result is something that looks both ethnic and sophisticated.

Supported by the Singapore Tourism Board, Mumbai Sé is a perfect venue for Indian haute couture, which is fast gaining an audience worldwide. Monthly themed in-store events are held to sustain cultural exchanges between India and Singapore, enriching the latter's cultural and social scene.

FACTS		
PRODUCTS	men's and women's fashion • art • jewellery • home décor • home furnishings	
FEATURES	contemporary and Indian fusion designs	
NEARBY	Orchard Road • Scotts Road • Tanglin Shopping Centre • bars • restaurants • city tours	
CONTACT	390 Orchard Road, #02-03 Palais Renaissance (opposite Hilton Hotel), Singapore 238871 • telephone: +65.6733 7188 • facsimile: +65.6733 6031 • email: pr@mumbai-se.com • website: www.mumbai-se.com	

PHOTOGRAPHS COURTESY OF MUMBAI SÉ.

Raoul

RAOUL offers a wide variety of shirts, tops and accessories for both men and women. Exquisite merchandise with affordable pricing in a trendy environment is what RAOUL is known and loved for by its fans in Asia and the Middle East.

Offering a wide range of styles, RAOUL makes it easy for customers who demand simplicity and quality. Here they can find the right shirt for any occasion, whether it's for work or play, casual or formal. Its functional yet stylish shirts and accessories make going from the office to after-work parties a breeze.

Woven in the same mills that produce fabrics for international luxury brands, the fabrics used for RAOUL's clothing line are of the highest quality. There are four varieties of fabrics to choose from at RAOUL; single-ply, Premium two-ply, Super four-ply and Indulgence.

Touted as the crème de la crème of all fabrics, Indulgence is known for its ultra fine material with an exquisite sheen. The shirts in the two-ply, four-ply and Indulgence categories all come with real mother-of-pearl buttons and custom cuffs.

Fine detailing and craftsmanship...

A range of comfortable and fashionable knits and sweaters for men is also available in various colours to complement the shirts. They are made from fabrics known for their luxurious appearance, softness and natural sheen.

RAOUL Men also offers an extensive range of accessories like ties, cufflinks, shoes, belts, watches, boxer shorts and a special Jetsetter luggage series, which all carry RAOUL's promise of exceptional quality.

The silk ties are all 100 per cent Italian-made, offered in the season's latest styles in an explosion of colours and a myriad of designs. Every season, RAOUL sources the style capitals of Europe for cufflinks to suit RAOUL's clientele. These cufflinks are crafted from quality materials such as crystals, semi-precious stones, sterling silver and rhodium.

RAOUL's range of leather goods combines function with style. The leather belts and shoes are manufactured in Italy, and are designed with comfort in mind.

RAOUL has recently launched its watch collection to further expand its accessories range. Fine detailing and craftsmanship are the elements that make the RAOUL watch a timeless accessory.

THIS PAGE (FROM TOP): Accessories that make a statement: imported cufflinks that make great gifts, belts imported from Italy, and watches to complete the look; RAOUL shoes, including these loafers are all made in Italy.

OPPOSITE: Clothing essentials for the stylish professional; RAOUL Men at Paragon Shopping Centre.

In addition, RAOUL offers a range of boxer shorts from the same fabric as its shirts, which is soft to the touch and very comfortable.

The RAOUL Ladies collection, which uses the same exquisite fabrics, is not only functional but is also highly versatile, to ensure that each piece can be styled easily to achieve different looks. Shirts with a new attitude and a new twist are what women can expect from RAOUL Ladies, which also features a collection of silk and cashmere knits, bustiers, halter neck blouses, camisoles and shirt dresses. From corporate sophisticated to smart casual or playful chic, there is something right for every woman.

RAOUL Ladies also carries accessories such as cufflinks, jewellery, shawls, scarves, chic bags and shoes. Its collection of exquisite jewellery includes earrings, rings, pendants, chokers, necklaces and brooches crafted in sterling silver with sparkling crystals and gems.

Targeted at both men and women, the RAOUL Jetsetter luggage series is designed for business travellers who are constantly on the go. Apart from the three-piece luggage consisting of a trolley bag, overnight bag and a laptop bag, RAOUL

...functionality, versatility and exceptional style.

has also thoughtfully designed travel accessories and kits such as a shirt organiser, shoe bag, accessory box, toiletry bag with waterproof compartment and a tube bag where clean and soiled socks and underwear can be stored separately on both ends. Since its launch, the Jetsetter luggage series has attracted a loyal following amongst travellers because of its functionality, versatility and exceptional style.

RAOUL updates its collections at a constant pace to keep abreast of international fashion trends to continually surprise its customers with fresher styles, giving loyal RAOUL patrons the added edge—by always being one step ahead of the fashion pack.

FACTS	
PRODUCTS	men's and women's fashion • fashion accessories • shoes • bags
FEATURES	assorted cuts and styles for cuffs and collars • Jetsetter luggage series for travellers
NEARBY	shopping • dining • sightseeing • city tours • cinema • fitness centre
CONTACT	290 Orchard Road, #02-02/03 and #02-12 Paragon Shopping Centre, Singapore 238859; telephone +65.6737 0682, +65.6737 9619 • 3 Temasek Boulevard #01-22/24 Suntec City Mall, Singapore 038983; telephone +65.6883 2589 • 9 Raffles Boulevard, #01-39/40 Millenia Walk, Singapore 039596; telephone +65.6837 2748 • 16 Collyer Quay, #01-11/12 Hitachi Tower, Singapore 049318; telephone +65.6538 3390 • RAOUL Men: Airport Boulevard, Changi Airport, #026-107-01 Departure Lounge Terminal 2 Building, Singapore 819643; telephone +65.6542 9660 • website: www.raoul.com

Risis

RISIS captures the beauty of Singapore's orchid collection in its exquisite 24K gold-plated fashion accessories. It first opened in 1976, and since then it has established itself as an award-winning company that produces unique, affordable and wearable art.

The Peranakan collection is RISIS' enduring series of jewellery. The range was inspired by the resplendent kerosangs of the Straits-born Chinese, otherwise referred to as the Peranakans. The kerosang is a three-piece brooch Peranakan women use to fasten their kebaya, or traditional blouse. The Peranakan collection is comprised of dragonflies, singing birds and intricate starburst patterns crafted in 925 sterling silver and finished in rhodium. The brooches also come with matching earrings.

Another notable collection is the Vanda, which is a modern take on the classic gilded orchid pieces. Like the Peranakan collection, the pieces are crafted in 925 sterling silver and finished with rhodium. Each of the stylised orchids in this collection cradle a pearl in the middle.

Asian themes figure prominently in RISIS jewellery, which is also inspired by other

...an award-winning company that produces unique, affordable and wearable art.

objects in nature such as ferns, leaves, fruits and roses. Apart from the themed jewellery collections, there are also accessories for men. RISIS' product range now extends beyond fashion accessories. It also creates elegant stationery, tableware and home décor such as figurines, picture frames and the 24K gold-plated Dial of Hope, a simplified feng shui compass. Paperweights, card holders, chopsticks, frames, trays and other desktop accessories make up its range of corporate gifts. Jewellery however, remains its main product.

Good craftsmanship and high production standards have earned RISIS a Certificate for Good Manufacturing Practice from the Singapore Institute of Standards and Industrial Research whose acronym, incidentally, is RISIS spelled backwards.

It also won the Singapore Design Award and the Best Tourism Souvenir award from the Singapore Tourism Board. Its popularity among tourists comes as no surprise.

RISIS has five exclusive boutiques, three of which are at Centrepoint, Suntec City and in the Singapore Botanic Gardens. Gift counters are also located along the Orchard Road shopping belt. Experienced sales personnel are well versed in the complicated production techniques and would be happy to explain how each unique piece is created.

RISIS also has a presence in international markets such as Paris, Hong Kong, Shanghai, New Jersey, Kuala Lumpur and Penang.

THIS PAGE (FROM LEFT): Pieces from the Vanda Light collection; Freedom Horse from the Zodiac line of corporate gifts.

OPPOSITE: The entire range of RISIS products, which also include the frames on the wall, are in well-lit shelves and display cases.

FACTS

PRODUCTS	24K gold-plated fashion accessories • home décor • corporate gifts
FEATURES	patented gold-plated, rhodium-plated and ruthenium-plated jewellery and accessories
NEARBY	Orchard Road • Takashimaya Shopping Centre • Dempsey Road • Tanglin Mall
CONTACT	#01-40 Centrepoint Shopping Centre, 176 Orchard Road, Singapore 238843 • RISIS, Suntec City Mall #01-084, Singapore 038983 • 1 Woodlands Square, Causeway Point #01-37, Singapore 738099 • Changi Airport Terminal 1 Departure/ Transit Lounge #021-43, Singapore 918141 • RISIS Nature Gallery, National Orchid Garden, Singapore Botanic Gardens, Cluny Road, Singapore 259569 • telephone: +65.6235 0988 (Centrepoint), +65.6338 8250 (Suntec City), +65.6893 9930 (Causeway Point), +65.6542 0220 (Changi Airport), +65.6835 2492, +65.6475 5104 (Botanic Gardens) • email: clientservice@risis.com.sg • website: www.risis.com

Tangs

At 74, Tangs is one of the premier shopping destinations in Singapore today. A prominent player in the vibrant Singapore retail arena, Tangs has always responded well to changing consumer trends and continually strives to break new ground and set new benchmarks within the industry through innovative store design, unique merchandising concepts, creative marketing and service excellence.

With a collection of specialty businesses spread over five levels, Tangs caters to the fashion and fashion-related lifestyle needs of its discerning contemporary shoppers. Merchandise is sourced from around the world, together

with its stable of private and exclusive labels, which are concept-themed and displayed according to specific lifestyles.

For the modern fashion elite, Tang+Co offers a comprehensive range of merchandise that promises "new luxury", with a complete and unique selection of international designer wear and all the finishing touches like must-have shoes, bags, accessories, and even beauty treats set in a new lifestyle boutique concept.

Located on Level 2, ladies can make their selections from more than 20 brands of international designer ready-to-wear ranging from Alannah Hill, Stella Forrest to Rebecca Taylor and Gorman, exquisite shoes and accessories collections from

THIS PAGE (FROM TOP): Tangs' distinctive facade; Find shoes, clothing and accessories from international brands at Tang+Co.

OPPOSITE (FROM TOP): Premium beauty products from Tang+Co Beauty; Dressing Room's different types and styles of lingerie suit every need, mood and personality; new collections are showcased at Trend Spot, located at the centre of Dressing Room.

Beverly Feldman, BCBG Girls, Salvador Sapena, Ras, Sambag, Luna and more.

To complete the coddling, at Tang+Co Beauty, shoppers will find premium home scents, collectible fragrances from Annick Goutal and L'Artisan Parfumeur as well as body and bath products from Molten Brown. One Beauty Place, Tang+Co Beauty's spa, completes the options for pampering and relaxation with its massage treatments, facials and other beauty services for men and women.

Similarly on Level 3, at Tang+Co Men, expect to find quality fashion collections from around the globe with exclusive labels such as Emporium Viri, Armand Basi, Coast and Arthur Galan. The discerning shopper will also find the irresistible Vertu luxury phones here.

The whole shopping experience at Tang+Co is enhanced with plush furnishings,

designer lighting, soothing music and exceptional service from Tang+Co Fashion Associates, who are equipped with all the latest trend tips and style advice whenever needed.

An award winning concept, Dressing Room on Level 2 is a girl's world of ultimate pampering and luxury as she shops for the most beautiful intimate apparel in a plush setting of a boudoir. The wide range of intimate apparel includes modern and chic lingerie from brands such as No Romeo and Hey Sister!; sexy feminine styles from O Lingerie; trendy designs from 6ixty 8ight

and Morgan; luxurious designs from brands like Elegantly Scant and Love & Lustre as well as practical foundation garments from Wacoal and Triumph.

Women will definitely be tickled as they step into the four themed fitting-rooms—Queen of Hearts (for the seductive lolita), Peek-A-Boo (for the cheeky girl), Luxe Deluxe (for the decadent vamp) and Pin-Up Girl (for the fun-loving girl). Velvet walls, fancy mirrors and mood lighting all set the tone for a unique experience.

At the centre of the women's fashion floor is Wardrobe—a collection of original fashion labels that include apparel, shoes, accessories and handbags, with a touch of individuality to differentiate itself from the onslaught of generic, global styles. It consists of building blocks to a great wardrobe, with brands such as Studio, Island Shop, Martina Pink, Moonstone, Woon Hung and Huer Gallery.

Men's fashion for business and leisure can be found in The Library, which is located on Level 3. It offers a comprehensive range of workwear, casual basics as well as a gamut of complimentary accessories like belts, ties, shoes, cuff links and writing instruments.

PlayLab, which is also on Level 3, is a one-stop station where shoppers can find the latest alternative trends—with exciting denim collections from G-Star, Levi's and Industrie to edgy, alternative labels such as Playhound, Marshall Artist, Grab; and sportswear from brands like Nike and Pony.

Playground is a fun, interactive and exciting fashion retail concept for kids located on Level 4. From miniature interpretations hot off the international runways and scaled-down classic fashion staples to functional yet chic baby accessories and creative toys, Playground offers an extensive range of fashion and lifestyle merchandise inspired by the latest adult trends. Ever mindful of its shoppers' every need, there is a private nursing lounge at Playground where parents can nurse their babies.

...all the best under one roof.

Island Café, on Level 4 was reopened in November 2005 to rave reviews for its new look and revamped menu selections. Diners can now enjoy a delectable dinning experience in a cosy, resort-like ambience while savouring Island Café's signature dishes and its wide variety of Asian-fusion cuisine.

As a testament to the unyielding efforts in the last couple of years to elevate the store's shopping experience through unique and differentiated lifestyle concepts, Tangs was presented with three prestigious awards—"Best Retail Concept of the Year" from the Singapore Retailers Association, "Best Shopping Experience – Department Store" and "Best New Retail Concept – Dressing Room" from the Singapore Tourism Board at the 20th Tourism Awards.

With a comprehensive range of merchandise and services to suit all of its shoppers' needs, Tangs truly provides all the best under one roof.

FACTS

PRODUCTS	men's, women's and children's fashion • fashion accessories • shoes • educational toys • electronic gadgets • homeware • kitchenware
FEATURES	personal shoppers • workshops • customised beauty programmes • parents' lounge • Island Bar Java • Island Café
NEARBY	shopping • dining • sightseeing • city tours • cinemas
CONTACT	310–320 Orchard Road, Singapore 238864 • telephone: +65.6737 5500 • facsimile: +65.6734 4714 • email: customer_service@tangs.com.sg • website: www.tangs.com

PHOTOGRAPHS COURTESY OF TANGS.

Wisma Atria

Occupying the most desirable spot in the heart of Orchard Road, Wisma Atria is a cosmopolitan lifestyle shopping destination that is literally in the centre of the action.

It has over 100 fashion shops and boutiques carrying the latest styles from exciting brands, and always offers something new that can't be found elsewhere. Wisma Atria is a comfortable shopping venue with friendly service, where women can find almost everything they are looking for at an affordable price.

There are 51 fashion boutiques spread across the mall's five levels. These include flagship tenants Topshop/Topman from England and Isetan Department Store from Japan, where Mango, DKNY, Levi's, Calvin Klein, Armani Jeans and Esprit are located. There are international brands such as FCUK, Karen Millen, Maxstudio.com, BCBGMAXAZRIA, Warehouse and bebe as well as shops that appeal to young professionals, such as Nine West, G2000, Paul & Joe,

Lacoste, Liz Claiborne and ALDO. Local brands such as prettyFIT, GG<5 and Daniel Yam carry stylish shoes, fashion and accessories from the country's own crop of talented designers.

Affordable casual wear and trendy accessories are available at Charles & Keith, Giordano, U2 and California-based brand Forever 21, whose shop in Wisma Atria is its only one in Singapore. Fila, Nike Women and Flash N Splash are some of the most popular sports fashion shops that carry beachwear, active wear and casual wear.

Timepieces from a wide range of styles and prices are offered at ALL WATCHES, City Chain, Dickson Watch, Red Army Watches and TAG Heuer. Diamonds and other precious gems that provide that elegant touch to an outfit

can be found in well-known jewellery boutiques such as Aspial, CITIGEMS, GOLDHEART, Lee Hwa and Soo Kee.

For the latest gadgets and sophisticated home appliances, shoppers can visit lifestyle concept stores such as Sony Gallery.

Wisma Atria received Superbrand status in the shopping centre category in the Superbrands Singapore Awards for 2004 and 2005, and has become the fashion savvy's destination of choice for shopping and dining.

Food Republic, its food atrium, introduces a new dining concept by combining 15 hawker stalls and 9 mini-restaurants. Some of the local food served at the hawker stalls are Hainanese chicken rice, curry rice, beef noodles, and roti prata.

THIS PAGE: Fashion choices for people who know what they want and are updated with the latest trends.
OPPOSITE: The "beautiful blue building", as Wisma Atria is sometimes referred to, is a shopping mecca for women.

...a must-visit for style experts and shoppers who are familiar with the latest trends.

(23,000-sq ft) space can comfortably accommodate 900 diners at a time.

Aromatic coffees, imported teas, freshly baked pastries, light snacks and healthy contemporary cuisine can be found in other establishments apart from the food court. C-Jade Express, Starbucks Coffee, Din Tai Fung, Ichiban Boshi, BreadTalk Transit, Famous Amos and PizzaWalker offer a wide range of dining choices in fashionable surroundings that appeal to the taste and preference of Wisma Atria's sophisticated shoppers.

IndoChine Wisma incorporating Nude + Supperclub, known for its ingeniously designed interiors and innovative Indo-chinese cuisine, and Sanctuary Garden, a

The mini-restaurants, on the other hand, offer Thai, North Indian, Peranakan, Cantonese, Japanese and Korean cuisine. Some of the popular dishes include north Indian fusion for meat lovers and vegetarians, Hong Kong-style roast duck, teppanyaki and American food.

Unlike the stark illumination and plastic furniture of most food centres, Food Republic has warm lighting and custom-made wood tables and chairs.

Its setup resembles a hawker centre back in the 1960s and 1970s, evoking a nostalgic ambience. Its 2,137-sq m

THIS PAGE: The trailblazing Food Republic serves modern cuisine in a nostalgic ambience; designer coffee at Starbucks.

OPPOSITE: Wisma Atria is a cosmopolitan lifestyle shopping destination; besides being a shopping mecca, the mall is also famous for its cuisine offerings.

With its varied fashion, dining and entertainment choices, Wisma Atria is truly a must-visit for style experts and seasoned shoppers who are familiar with the latest trends.

bar with live band performances, is a popular hangout. Another al fresco dining option is Cosmopolitan Bar & Caffe that offers an engaging mix of international cuisines.

True to its commitment to continuous innovation, Wisma Atria is the only shopping centre along Orchard Road that offers concierge services.

Tourists and shoppers can charge their mobile phones, place restaurant reservations, collect GST refunds, book city tours and buy SISTIC tickets for concerts and musicals with the concierge, who may recommend itineraries based on one's tour and entertainment preferences. Airline tickets may also be reconfirmed here.

FACTS

PRODUCTS	international brands • dining, lifestyle and entertainment outlets
FEATURES	concierge services for tourists • unique dining concept
NEARBY	Orchard Road • Scotts Road • Marriott Hotel • Meritus Mandarin • Grand Hyatt • Hilton Singapore • Ngee Ann City • bars and restaurants • city tours
CONTACT	435 Orchard Road, Singapore 238877 • telephone: +65.6235 2103 • facsimile: +65.6733 4037 • email: concierge@macquariepacificstar.com • website: www.wismaonline.com

PHOTOGRAPHS COURTESY OF WISMA ATRIA.

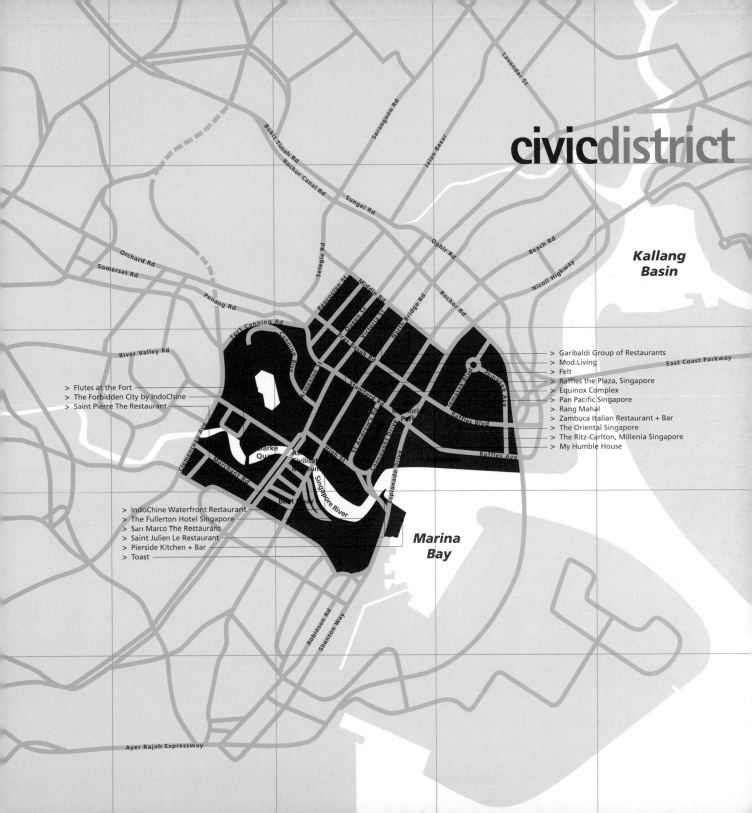

civicdistrict

Kallang Basin

Marina Bay

East Coast Parkway

Lavender St
Bukit Timah Rd
Rochor Canal Rd
Serangoon Rd
Jalan Besar
Sungei Rd
Ophir Rd
Beach Rd
Nicoll Highway
Orchard Rd
Somerset Rd
Penang Rd
Fort Canning Rd
River Valley Rd
Bencoolen St
Middle Rd
Queen St
Victoria St
Prinsep St
Cairnhill Rise
Armenian St
North Bridge Rd
Rochor Rd
Stamford Rd
Temasek Ave
Raffles Blvd
Raffles Ave
Selegie Rd
Coleman St
St Andrew's Rd
High St
Connaught Drive
Esplanade Drive
Esplanade
Victoria Park
Merchant Rd
Clemenceau Ave
Boat Quay
Singapore River
Clarke Quay
Asian Civilisations Museum
Robinson Rd
Shenton Way
Ayer Rajah Expressway

> Flutes at the Fort
> The Forbidden City by IndoChine
> Saint Pierre The Restaurant

> IndoChine Waterfront Restaurant
> The Fullerton Hotel Singapore
> San Marco The Restaurant
> Saint Julien Le Restaurant
> Pierside Kitchen + Bar
> Toast

> Garibaldi Group of Restaurants
> Mod.Living
> Felt
> Raffles the Plaza, Singapore
> Equinox Complex
> Pan Pacific Singapore
> Rang Mahal
> Zambuca Italian Restaurant + Bar
> The Oriental Singapore
> The Ritz-Carlton, Millenia Singapore
> My Humble House

singapore, past and present

In some ways, the area around the mouth of the Singapore River hasn't
changed much over the past 180 years. It was here, in the river's northern
bank, that Sir Stamford Raffles first set foot in Singapore. And it was in this
area that he decided to build Singapore's city centre. The 1822 city plan
specified that the commercial district would be to the south of the river while
the administrative offices would be to the north. Today, the city's financial
centres—Raffles Place and Shenton Way—are south of the river. While the
colonial buildings that once housed the country's government are still standing
north of the river, most of the ministries and other government offices have long
since relocated to new and more modern premises in different parts of the island.
This area, though, is still very much one of country's most important, most populated
and most exciting parts of Singapore.

 The civic district is where Singapore's past and present sit side by side.
Colonial buildings are surrounded by sleek glass and steel skyscrapers, luxury
hotels, shopping centres and rows of restaurants and pubs in refurbished
shophouses. In this area, one can find religious sites, financial institutions,
government ministries and agencies, high-end electronics shops, clubs, arts
centres, galleries—and even a Parisian nude revue.

the centre of activity

The core of the civic district is the Padang, which in Malay literally translates to
'playing field'. This grass patch opposite the old Supreme Court and City Hall was
once the venue of the country's most important sporting events. Today, aside from the
occasional National Day parade, it is mostly used by the Singapore Recreation Club
and the Singapore Cricket Club, which each own half of the field. The Padang, like
so much of the civic district, was once a seafront location. It is now over 1 km
(0.6 miles) away from the ocean because of land reclamation.

PAGE 102: *The spikey domes of
the Esplanade—Theatres on the
Bay have become a famous
landmark in Singapore.*

THIS PAGE (FROM TOP): *After the buzz
of the office crowd in the
morning, all is quiet at Raffles
Place in the afternoon;
the Padang is a favourite venue
for sports like cricket and rugby.*

OPPOSITE: *The coexistence of old
and new—the shophouses give
a nostalgic feel to the bustling
financial district filled with
gleaming skyscrapers.*

seats of government

Opposite the Padang are City Hall and the former Supreme Court. The site where the latter sits was once that of the posh and exclusive Hotel de L'Europe. In 2005, the Ministry of Information, Communications and the Arts announced plans to convert these neoclassical buildings into a new national arts gallery, which it hopes will become Southeast Asia's premiere visual arts space. This new museum will exhibit the works of important artists from the region and the rest of the world.

The new Supreme Court building, which opened in 2005, is located just behind City Hall. This marble behemoth designed by Sir Norman Foster is easily recognisable because of its UFO-shaped structure on top. Most of the courts are closed to the public, but the lobby and the law academy's bistro on the first floor are open to visitors. Jimmy Chok, who runs The Academy Bistro, is one of the city's most respected young chefs.

centres of culture

The colonial buildings south of the Padang are all dedicated to the arts. What is now known as Victoria Concert Hall was formerly named Victoria Memorial Hall, a tribute to Queen Victoria. The conjoined Victoria Theatre served as the original town hall. These two buildings were the city's main performing arts venues before Esplanade—Theatres on the Bay opened in 2002.

Next to Victoria Theatre and Concert Hall is the Old Parliament House, built in 1827 as the private residence of a businessman. It was a neo-Palladian structure designed by G.D. Coleman, the architect who designed most of the country's civil infrastructure. Although much of its original design was lost through major alterations in 1901 and again in 1953, it remains as the country's oldest government building.

In 1999, the parliament moved to a larger, more modern home just a street away. The Old Parliament House was reopened in 2004 as an arts centre and renamed The Arts House. It has performance halls, a theatre, a visual arts exhibition area, a gallery shop specialising in locally made crafts, a retail store dedicated to local literature and

THIS PAGE (FROM LEFT): *The Parliament House's signature prism-shaped top was designed by the late former President of Singapore, Ong Teng Cheong; the UFO-shaped structure on top of the new Supreme Court designed by Sir Norman Foster makes the building distinctive.*

OPPOSITE: *With its Corinthian columns and classical design, the old Supreme Court building is indeed a majestic structure.*

music, a café, and function rooms that are available for private or corporate events. The main parliamentary chamber has been preserved and makes for one of Singapore's most unique stages. An annex of The Arts House contains a restaurant and a modern bar.

Just south of The Arts House and sitting along the Singapore River is Empress Place Building. The beautiful structure was constructed in the 1860s to serve as a courthouse, and has had four major additions since then. Today, it houses one of the region's premier museums, the Asian Civilisations Museum. It holds some of the most stunning exhibitions that showcase the diverse histories of Pan-Asian cultures. In addition to the museum, the building also has a hip café, chic restaurant and swanky bar, which are all popular among the city's elites. The Substation, which occupies a former power station, is a contemporary art centre in Armenian Street. Artists, curators and art lovers use the space to interact and exhibit.

Apart from critically acclaimed writers and intellectuals, The Substation also works with emerging artists. Also along this street is the Asian Civilisation Museum, Armenian Street, and it specialises in showcasing the culture and history of the Peranakans, otherwise known as the Straits Chinese. Presently closed, it is undergoing a transformation to become a full-fleged boutique Peranakan Museum, which is expected to reopen again in a few years time.

The National Museum of Singapore on Stamford Road, which was previously known as the Singapore History Museum, originally housed the Raffles Museum and Library that was built in 1887, and was known for its collection on natural history of Southeast Asia. It was renamed National Museum in 1969, and its focus shifted to collections that reflected Singapore's nation-building stance. Now, the museum has undergone extensive renovation, and has been expanded to more than double its current size to make room for new galleries and more venues for talks, screenings and performances.

Sitting on Bras Basah Road to the east of the National Museum of Singapore is the Singapore Art Museum, which reportedly has one of the world's best collections of Southeast Asian art. It is located in the grounds of St. Joseph's Institution, one of Singapore's oldest Catholic boys' school. The Singapore Philatelic Museum is one of Singapore's smallest museums. Located in Canning Rise, it resides in the former Methodist Book Room building. Most visitors usually would not think of putting a stamp museum in their itineraries, but this museum has done an excellent job of holding exhibitions that make the subject of stamp collecting interesting to just about anyone. Its collection of postal artefacts, which includes rare stamps from the 18th century, traces Singapore's postal history and its development as a country.

ABOVE: Prickly-looking on the outside but acoustically spectacular on the inside, the Esplanade—Theatres on the Bay is an arts centre that makes an impact.

OPPOSITE: The Singapore Symphony Orchestra performs more than 50 concerts a year.

In the Marina Bay area is Esplanade—Theatres on the Bay. Opened on October 12, 2002, it was jointly designed by two achitectural firms, the London-based Michael Wilford & Partners and DP Architects Pte Ltd. This structure is hard to miss—some say they resemble a fly's eyes while others say they look like twin durians. However, the design of the famous twin domes are inspired by neither. Instead, the reason for their spikey appearances is because the exterior is made from 7,139 variously angled aluminium shades that maximise natural light while shielding the glass roof from sun and heat. Nevertheless, with an estimated land value and building costs that amounted to a whopping S$1 billion, it was intended to do two things: to create a tourist attraction similar to the Sydney Opera House, and to provide a state-of-the-art concert hall and theatre. The Esplanade, which also houses rehearsal studios, a visual arts exhibition space and an extension of the National Library, has held performances by the world's best performing arts groups and hosted productions of some of Singapore's best troupes.

Theatreworks, a notable performing arts group, nurtures local talent and supports Singaporean writing through its productions and development programmes. The group's artistic director, Ong Keng Sen, is best known in local and international theatre circles for creating a new genre called docu-performance.

Singapore Symphony Orchestra (SSO) performs regularly, often with foreign guests, at either Victoria Concert Hall or the Esplanade. Formed in 1979, the SSO used to be housed at Victoria Concert Hall until it moved to the new Esplanade Concert Hall in 2002. In an attempt to make classical music more accessible to the public, the SSO has organised free outdoor concerts for the masses. Another noteworthy group is the Singapore Chinese Orchestra. In addition to the Symphony Orchestra and the Chinese Orchestra, easily the country's two largest and most important music groups, Singapore is home to many other musicians, ranging from pop talents to jazz ensembles, baroque quartets and classical musicians.

Visual arts lovers should consider coming to Singapore in the fall of even years.

The Singapore Dance Theatre, the most well-known dance troupe in town and Fort Canning Centre's resident ballet company, performs both classical and contemporary pieces. It has toured internationally and received rave reviews. Locals flock to their regular free outdoor performances, dubbed "Ballet Under the Stars".

In addition to the many exceptional museums, art galleries and exhibition areas in the civic district, the other non-commercial spaces especially worth visiting are The Substation, mentioned previously, and the Institute of Contemporary Arts Singapore (ICA Singapore), established by the LASELLE-SIA College of the Arts. The ICA Singapore, along with its parent university, will be moving to a new campus come 2007, where it will boast Singapore's largest art gallery. Visitors who plan on touring the city's galleries should also include the Ministry of Information, Communications and the Arts (MICA) building in their itinerary. This former police station, it is home to its eponymous ministry, as well as several MICA-related agencies, including the National Heritage Board and the National Arts Council—the agencies in charge of applied arts, museums and heritage, and the fine arts.

Interested visitors can get a full picture of Singapore's art scene in June, during its dynamic, month-long Singapore Arts Festival. This annual arts festival has been going on for almost 30 years, and has brought together some of the world's best performing arts groups. The festival, in association with other festivals from around the world, also commissions new work by both local and international groups. Visual arts lovers should consider coming to Singapore in the fall of even years. In September 2006, the National Arts Council will launch Singapore Biennale 2006, Singapore's first international contemporary visual arts exhibition. The first exhibition will be curated by Fumio Nanjo, the deputy director of the Mori Art Museum in Tokyo. Foreign artists such as Jenny Holzer, Eduardo Kac and Mariko Mori will be joined by young Singaporean artists. Apart from these two festivals, which are run and funded by the government, there are other noteworthy ones that are organised by arts groups and the private sector. These include

THIS PAGE (FROM TOP): The Singapore Biennale will bring together over 80 artists from more than 50 countries; the Singapore Art Museum has the largest collection of Southeast Asian art; the Singapore Dance Theatre brings ballet to the masses through its Ballet Under the Stars shows.
OPPOSITE: The MICA building's colourful windows reflect the vibrancy of the nation's burgeoning arts scene.

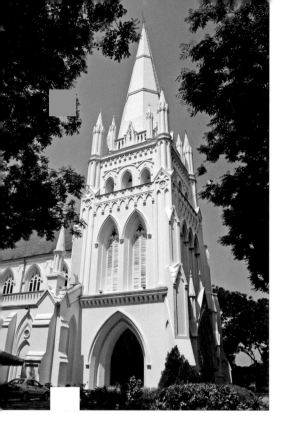

the M1 Singapore Fringe Festival; Mosaic, a jazz and world music festival organised by the Esplanade; and World of Music, Arts and Dance, or WOMAD. Event listings are available in *The Straits Times* or *I-S Magazine*, a weekly freesheet.

historical places of worship

Just north of the old City Hall is St Andrew's Cathedral, an Anglican Church designed by Colonel Ronald MacPherson in 1856. This brilliant, all-white neo-Gothic structure was opened and consecrated in January 1862, and built by Indian convict labour imported by the British. The original church, designed by G.D. Coleman, was demolished by lightning in 1852.

A few steps north of the Philatelic Museum, between Victoria and Armenian Streets, is the small and beautiful Armenian Church of St. Gregory the Illuminator. It was also designed by G.D. Coleman and was completed in 1835. One of the oldest buildings in Singapore, this historic church is also a great testament to the early Armenian immigrants who were instrumental in helping to develop Singapore in the 19th century. The grounds also contain a small residential house and a small graveyard. History buffs and orchid lovers will be interested to know that the grave of Agnes Joaquim, the Armenian for whom Singapore's national flower was named after, is here. During the 19th century, Joaquim discovered a pretty, purple flower in her garden and had it registered at the Botanic Gardens. Since then, the bloom became known as the Vanda Miss Joaquim orchid.

landmarks

In front of Victoria Theatre and Concert Hall is a bronze statue of Sir Stamford Raffles, the man who founded Singapore. A replica located between Empress Place and The Arts House marks the spot where, in January 1819, Raffles first set foot on the island. Another famous landmark is Raffles Hotel along Bras Basah Road. What is now a sprawling property with 103 suites, over a half dozen restaurants and

THIS PAGE (FROM TOP): St Andrew's Cathedral is a well-loved place of worship; the Vanda Miss Joaquim orchid is Singapore's national flower.

OPPOSITE (FROM TOP): The Civilian War Memorial was built to remember the victims of World War II; the central business district forms an impressive backdrop to two icons, the merlion and The Fullerton Hotel.

upscale shops which include Louis Vuitton humbly began as bunglow owned by Arab trader Mohamed Alsagoff. The Sarkies brothers, the Armenian hoteliers who also built the Eastern & Oriental Hotel in Penang and The Strand Hotel in Rangoon, purchased the property in 1886. The hotel officially opened on December 1, 1887 and has since set the benchmark for grace and luxury in Singapore. Among its frequent visitors are international celebrities, writers and aristocrats. Joseph Conrad, Rudyard Kipling, Somerset Maugham and Noel Coward were just some of the sterling writers who stayed at the hotel. Queen Elizabeth II graced its rooms, as did famous movie stars Charlie Chaplin, Ava Gardner, Jean Harlow and Elizabeth Taylor. Thanks to its multi-million-dollar facelift in 1989, Raffles Hotel remains one of Singapore's most impressive hotels and important buildings.

Along the river, directly across Cavenagh Bridge is another icon, The Fullerton Hotel. Built in 1928, this neoclassical building served as the country's General Post Office for decades.

The Civilian War Memorial opposite Raffles City Shopping Centre was built in 1967 to commemorate the victims of the Japanese Occupation. Locals fondly refer to the 61-m (200-ft) monument made of four identical stone towers as "chopsticks".

modern icons

Across the historical Raffles Hotel is one of Singapore's most modern icons, Raffles City. This shopping centre was designed by I.M. Pei, one of the masters of modernist architecture best known for The Louvre Pyramid in Paris. It opened in 1985 and comprises an office tower, shopping mall and two hotels—Raffles the Plaza and Swissôtel the Stamford. The Westin Stamford, now the Swissôtel the Stamford, was the tallest hotel in the world when it first opened.

The Marina Bay area lies directly to the west. This area, built entirely on reclaimed land, is home to the Suntec Convention Centre, several office buildings, three shopping centres and four fantastic hotels. The world's largest fountain, the Fountain of Wealth, is at the centre of the five-building Suntec Convention Centre. A tourist attraction by itself, the fountain draws a great number of tourists and locals who believe touching its water will bring them good luck and prosperity.

dining destinations and night life

Singapore certainly knows how to let its hair down after dark. Whether it's a loud, crowded, crazy club or a sleek jazz bar, Singapore is jam-packed with options.

CHIJMES, pronounced "chimes", is a complex of restaurants, pubs and shops. It occupies what used to be the Convent of the Holy Infant Jesus. The convent occupied the area until 1983, after which the property—with its neo-Gothic architecture, courtyard, lawns, and covered walkways—was developed with the idea of transforming it into a Singaporean version of London's Covent Garden. However, it has never been able to draw enough people to become a real hotspot; CHIJMES is now primarily a dining destination.

At Empress Place, the café, Indochinese restaurant and bar—Siem Reap, IndoChine Waterfront and Bar Opiume respectively—are favourites of the city's elite. On cool nights, this is an excellent place for al fresco wining and dining by the river. Bar Opiume is particularly a much-favoured venue for intimate parties.

Zouk is the most popular nightspot, and has been so for more than a decade and a half. Its status as Singapore's number one club has recently been challenged by the Ministry of Sound, a branch of the world-renowned British dance club of the same name, which opened in December 2005.

For those more inclined to drinking and talking than dancing, Mohamed Sultan, Boat Quay, Clarke Quay and Emerald Hill are all popular watering holes. Mohamed Sultan was once a small one-lane side street with a few small bars. At the time, it was a journalists' hangout—the first bar on the street, Front Page, was owned by an ex-newspaper editor. Today this laid-back lane is now a bustling entertainment zone. The road has been widened to four lanes. Almost every unit along this busy road is occupied by a crowded popular bar. Its habitués have also changed, becoming much younger over the years; it is now a favourite weekend destination of university students and people in their early twenties.

Boat Quay, just off Raffles Place, started out as a small row of restaurants and pubs in restored shophouses along the river. It is such a popular venue that restaurants and pubs have spilled over onto the neighbouring streets. Upper Circular Road behind Boat

Quay is especially choked with busy bars, restaurants and cafés. Across the river is Clarke Quay. A much larger development than Boat Quay, this restored warehouse and shophouse area was originally meant to cater to families, while Boat Quay was targeted at urban professionals. Clarke Quay's client mix prior to a massive re-evaluation and renovation in 2005 was an odd potpourri of offices, lifestyle shops, galleries, restaurants, bars, and hawker stalls. In 2005, however, Clarke Quay was transformed into a nightlife zone. The Ministry of Sound is another one of the newest establishments in this area. Clarke Quay's most notable new tenant is Crazy Horse Paris, the French all-nude revue that raised more than just a few eyebrows when it opened here. The psychedelic light show teases the audience with its tantalising, peek-a-boo effect on the ladies during the performances.

a new entertainment concept

The "integrated resort", or IR for short, has been, and still is, a hot topic for debate in the political arena and public forums for the past year or so, ever since the government gave the green light to develop two IRs with casinos. Some feared the negative social impact casino gambling will have on Singaporeans, while some felt that the IRs will give a great boost to the local economy.

The Las Vegas Sands, which owns the Venetian Resort Casino Hotel in Las Vegas and Sands Macau, recently won the bid to develop the IR in the Marina Bay area. Its Marina Bay Sands will occupy approximately 21 hectares (52 acres) of the reclaimed waterfront land facing downtown Singapore. The mammoth project includes an art and science museum, six signature restaurants with celebrity chefs, three hotel towers with more than 2,000 rooms, a convention centre that could accommodate over 52,000 people, massive retail space and a waterfront promenade.

Sentosa, a small island south of Singapore, has also been earmarked for the development of the second IR. With hotels, restaurants, shopping, convention space, theatres, museums, theme parks and casinos all in one complex, these IRs aim to attract hundreds of visitors per year when they open in 2010.

THIS PAGE (FROM TOP): **The Ministry of Sound is quickly gaining ground in the party scene; groove and move to the beat at this international club.**

OPPOSITE: **At Crazy Horse Paris, the ladies bare all tastefully with a colourful light show.**

Clarke Quay's most notable new tenant is Crazy Horse Paris.

The Fullerton Hotel Singapore

The Fullerton Hotel Singapore is a marriage of tradition and modernity. It is a magnificent structure that preserves the island state's rich colonial history while offering its clients a luxurious stay and access to everything modern Singapore has to offer.

Completed in 1928, The Fullerton was once home to the General Post Office, the Chamber of Commerce and The Singapore Club, before it was redesigned as a luxury hotel. The Fullerton is an example of Palladian architecture, with tall Doric columns and grand porte-cochères. The hotel's interior is stylish and contemporary, yet still pays

THIS PAGE (FROM TOP): The hotel's interiors are furnished with contemporary pieces; one can still see the original ceiling of the General Post Office at the Post Bar.

OPPOSITE: Each room has high-speed Internet access and other amenities to meet the needs of leisure and business travellers.

homage to its architectural roots. The lobby's high ceiling creates an impression of limitless space. Contemporary art pieces provide a contrast to the classic interiors.

There are 400 rooms and suites which either overlook the sunlit atrium courtyard, or face stunning views of downtown Singapore's skyline, the river promenade or the sea. Bathrooms come complete with Fullerton Fundamentals, the hotel's signature line of bathroom amenities.

The crème de la crème of The Fullerton's accommodations is the 199-sq m (2,142-sq ft) Presidential Suite, which is accessed through its own elevator. The Suite's glass-enclosed veranda provides an ideal location for private dinners.

...a marriage of tradition and modernity.

Designed with the business and leisure traveller in mind, The Fullerton offers facilities that cater beautifully to both. There is a 24-hour Financial Centre with the Bloomberg Professional service providing up-to-the moment financial reports and world news, and meeting rooms equipped with the latest technologies. For leisure, there is an outdoor infinity-edge pool, fitness centre and spa.

Apart from The Courtyard, the hotel's lobby lounge which serves afternoon tea and offers a selection of premium blends and beverages, there are restaurants specialising in different types of cuisine. One can enjoy international dishes in a smart casual setting at Town Restaurant, modern Chinese specialties at Jade and Italian cuisine at the fine dining restaurant San Marco at The Lighthouse.

Standing at the mouth of the Singapore River, The Fullerton greets all boats that enter the city. Its prime location in Raffles Place is at the crux of Singapore's business, financial and cultural districts. The Singapore headquarters of all major banks are within walking distance, as are theatres, a concert hall, a museum and the Raffles Place MRT station. Boat Quay, one of the major food and entertainment districts, is a stroll away. The combination of modern facilities, thoughtful amenities and personalised service has won The Fullerton major travel and architectural awards such as the *Condé Nast Traveler* Gold List award and the Architectural Heritage Award from Singapore's Urban Redevelopment Authority.

FACTS		
ROOMS	379 rooms • 21 suites • 15 meeting rooms	
FOOD	Town Restaurant: international • Jade: modern Chinese • San Marco: modern Italian • Post Express Deli: gourmet delicatessen	
DRINK	The Courtyard: lobby lounge • Post Bar: martinis and cocktails	
FEATURES	outdoor infinity-edge pool • fitness centre • limousine hire • jogging route • 24-hour full-service business office • Bloomberg Professional service • high-speed and wireless Internet access • disabled access • shopping gallery • babysitting service	
NEARBY	business district • Boat Quay • Esplanade – Theatres on the Bay • museum	
CONTACT	1 Fullerton Square, Singapore 049178 • telephone: +65.6733 8388 • facsimile: +65.6735 8388 • email: info@fullertonhotel.com • website: www.fullertonhotel.com	

PHOTOGRAPHS COURTESY OF THE FULLERTON HOTEL SINGAPORE.

The Oriental Singapore

The Oriental Singapore's fan-shaped building is a stunning landmark at the waterfront of Marina Bay. Each of the guest rooms offers views of Singapore's skyline, harbour or the ocean.

The plush, modern rooms have wireless high-speed Internet access, cable and satellite television and intelligent air-conditioning and lighting systems. In addition, the Harbour and Ocean Rooms, Suites and Club Rooms are fitted with surround sound systems with CD/DVD options. The Oriental Club Lounge provides exclusive services to Club Floor guests, including complimentary champagne breakfasts, afternoon tea and evening cocktails, free local calls and bookings for performances at Esplanade – Theatres on the Bay.

Meeting facilities include the Oriental Ballroom, which can accommodate 600 persons, and 13 other meeting rooms.

Designed for the grandest of occasions, the ballroom is replete with splendid fixtures and handcrafted fabrics. As a venue for magnificent weddings, it is equipped with intelligent lighting systems and a state-of-the-

THIS PAGE (FROM TOP): Spa treatments and amenities that have earned the Mandarin Oriental chain of luxury hotels and resorts a reputation for having some of the best spas in the world; The Oriental Singapore combines oriental heritage with modern living.

OPPOSITE (FROM LEFT): Famous for its food, the hotel has five restaurants that offer various cuisines from all over the world; freshly baked goods on display at Melt – The World Café.

...the best in Asian hospitality and service...

The premium Oriental Spa features a private relaxation lounge, a yoga studio and a fitness studio. In keeping with The Mandarin Oriental's ethos, the restorative treatments here combine ancient philosophies with modern techniques, using 100 per cent pure essential oils and herbs.

The Oriental offers the best in Asian hospitality and service combined with cutting-edge technology and modern amenities—a place where one can experience classic elegance with contemporary convenience.

art surround sound system. Couples can go over setup options as well as wedding packages at the Bridal Salon, where a consultant is on hand to provide assistance.

No stay is complete without sampling gastronomic delights from the hotel's famous restaurants. Cherry Garden's haute Chinese cuisine has provincial touches. Dolce Vita offers relaxed Mediterranean dining by the pool. Its menu features the best from Southern Europe and North Africa, and has a stellar wine list to match. The large open kitchen that is its centrepiece puts the chefs in a perennial goldfish bowl.

Melt – The World Café introduces an innovative dining experience: diners walk around a multicultural food market, choose dishes and discuss the finer points of each with the chefs.

The Axis Bar and Lounge is a hip place to enjoy afternoon tea on a weekday or a cocktail in the evening with a view of the bay.

FACTS		
ROOMS	449 rooms • 78 suites	
FOOD	Melt – The World Café: international • Cherry Garden: haute Chinese • Dolce Vita: Mediterranean • Morton's, The Steakhouse: American • Wasabi Bistro: contemporary Japanese • Axis Bar and Lounge: afternoon tea	
DRINK	Axis Bar and Lounge • Morton's The Bar	
FEATURES	fitness studio • pool • bridal salon • spa • limousine hire • conferencing systems • business centre • wireless high-speed Internet access • ballroom • 13 meeting rooms	
NEARBY	business and financial district • shopping • theatre • museums • entertainment • dining • sightseeing • city tour	
CONTACT	5 Raffles Avenue, Singapore 039797 • telephone: +65.6338 0066 • facsimile: +65.6339 9537 • email: orsin@mohg.com • website: www.mandarinoriental.com	

PHOTOGRAPHS COURTESY OF THE ORIENTAL SINGAPORE.

Pan Pacific Singapore

Chic luxury, superb service and 37 storeys of spectacular views are but some of the promises of Pan Pacific Singapore. Others are elegantly appointed rooms, state-of-the-art facilities and a memorable experience that is unique to Pan Pacific.

Located in the heart of Marina Bay, the hotel lies in the midst of shopping malls such as Millenia Walk, Marina Square and Suntec Singapore International Convention & Exhibition Centre. The hotel is only minutes from the central business district and international airport.

For the finest in service and facilities, the Pacific Floor is unparalleled. A preferred venue for discerning travellers, the space is characterised by contemporary elegance and stylish décor, complemented by a dedicated team offering attentive, round-the-clock service. Each guestroom is lined with a plush Axminster striped carpet, its cheerful hue enhancing the designer touches that adorn the generous space. From the Herman Miller ergonomic task chair to the stress-relieving Hansgrohe massage showerhead in the marbled shower, an extensive pillow menu and a host of guest privileges, Pan Pacific Singapore has established service standards that encourage guests to make consecutive return visits.

Guests have a choice of Deluxe and Panoramic Rooms spread over more than 30 floors. The soothing colours in the rooms are complemented with bold splashes of green and black, and the wonderful array of in-room features like cable TV and high-speed Internet access promise all the conveniences of home and more.

THIS PAGE (FROM TOP): *Rooms provide stunning views of the sea and the city, as well as the swimming pool on the 4th floor; each room is equipped with modern luxuries, such as high-speed Internet connectivity, for the convenience of busy business travellers; hotel guests can relax with a cocktail at Keyaki Bar.*

OPPOSITE: *Pan Pacific's elegant lobby lounge invites guests to have a quiet drink away from the hustle and bustle of the city.*

Gastronomes will love the array of dining options available. Fans of Chinese food will be dazzled by Hai Tien Lo, the hotel's signature, multi-award winning Chinese restaurant which can be reached by the hotel's trademark bubble lift. The exquisite Cantonese cuisine, stunning chinoiserie décor, and panoramic views of the city and harbour all serve to create an unforgettable dining experience.

The hotel's renowned Japanese, Indian and Italian restaurants as well as its international dining outlet, Summer House, are extremely popular, and reservations are strongly recommended.

To get a healthy dose of fitness in body, mind and soul, there's the beautiful semi-circular Wellness Village, featuring complete spa and fitness facilities. The healing hands of highly-skilled therapists pamper guests from top to toe, a soothing treat after taking the yoga, Pilates and kickboxing classes available at the hotel's exercise studio.

PHOTOGRAPHS COURTESY OF PAN PACIFIC SINGAPORE.

FACTS		
ROOMS	737 rooms • 38 suites
FOOD	Keyaki Restaurant: Japanese • Summer House: international • Hai Tien Lo: Cantonese • Zambuca Italian Restaurant and Bar: Italian • Rang Mahal: Indian
DRINK	Wine Vault • The Atrium • Cabanas • Keyaki Bar
FEATURES	Wellness Village • pool • gym • tennis courts • spa
BUSINESS	high-speed Internet access • business suites
NEARBY	Suntec Singapore International Convention & Exhibition Centre • Millenia Walk • Marina Square Shopping Centre • Esplanade – Theatres on the Bay
CONTACT	Pan Pacific Singapore, 7 Raffles Boulevard, Marina Square, Singapore 039595 • telephone: +65.6336 8111 • facsimile: +65.6339 0382 • email: reserve.sin@panpacific.com • website: www.singapore.panpacific.com

Raffles The Plaza, Singapore

THIS PAGE (FROM TOP): *From designer bathroom fittings and luxurious bed linen to dining pleasures, everything is top-of-the-range in this world-class hotel.*

OPPOSITE: *RafflesAmrita Spa, which offers an extensive range of treatments and therapies, is one of the largest spas in Asia.*

Fancy a night or two in an ultra luxe suite which made the international 'Decadent Finds' list of *Elite Traveler* magazine? Raffles The Plaza has three penthouse suites that rank among the top in luxury accommodations around the world.

Each of these unique suites at Raffles The Plaza is conceptualised as an exclusive sanctuary for its residents. Its interiors and furnishings are designed to reflect a distinctive lifestyle—from the carefully selected art collection, library of books and wines in the cellar, to the thoughtfully equipped bathroom decked with luxurious RafflesAmrita Spa private label bath products. Every well-appointed guest-room features a bathroom with rainforest showerheads, high-speed Internet access, a spacious workstation, Bose sound system and a private balcony.

Over the years, Raffles The Plaza has won multiple awards, and infinitely more hearts, for its chic interiors, innovative dining concepts and superb service. The hotel is dressed with designer fittings in both public and guest areas, and residents are provided a quiet haven with the finest and legendary Raffles experience during their stay.

For the travelling gourmand, it's time to embark on a journey of epicurean delights, uncovering a myriad of tantalising dining, wining and entertainment choices as the hotel presents a collection of its signature restaurants and bars.

At RafflesAmrita Spa, pampering takes on a whole new meaning. Designed to

Each of these unique suites…is conceptualised as an exclusive sanctuary for its residents.

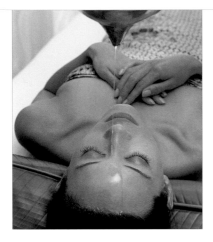

deliver bliss, relaxation and rejuvenation, the spa offers an exceptional variety of therapies and treatments on its extensive menu. The name, 'Amrita,' means 'elixir of youth' in Sanskrit, alluding to the beauty and health secrets that await behind its doors. At RafflesAmrita Spa, guests can look forward to being soothed, smoothed, restored and revived from head to toe.

This 4,600 sq m (49,513 sq ft) spa is spread over three levels, and has over 35 treatment rooms. Couples will enjoy the VIP couple suites, which come with in-room dining, private jacuzzi and an aromatherapy steam room. There are also pavilion couple suites by the swimming pools for those who prefer a communal spa setting.

Guests who prefer something more invigorating can head to the state-of-the-art gym, or attend the yoga, tai chi or Pilates classes offered.

FACTS		
ROOMS	769 guestrooms and suites • 3 penthouse suites	
FOOD	Prego Restaurant & Deli: Italian • Inagiku: Japanese • Equinox Restaurant: Asian and western • Jaan: modern French	
DRINK	INK Club Bar • Introbar • Lobby Court • City Space • New Asia Bar	
FEATURES	24-hour check-in/check-out services • RafflesAmrita Spa • gym • 2 pools	
BUSINESS	high-speed Internet access • business centre	
NEARBY	Raffles City Shopping Centre • Chijmes • CityLink Mall • Millennia Walk • Suntec Singapore International Convention & Exhibition Centre	
CONTACT	80 Bras Basah Road, Singapore 189560 • telephone: +65.6339 7777 • facsimile: +65.6337 1554 • email: reservations.plaza@raffles.com • website: www.singapore-plaza.raffles.com	

The Ritz-Carlton, Millenia Singapore

THIS PAGE (FROM TOP): *Room with a view—a tranquil space in the heart of the city; enjoy desserts like this sweet dumpling served with red date sweet soup at the Summer Pavilion Cantonese Restaurant.*

OPPOSITE: *Some of Singapore's best musicians play live jazz at the cosy Chihuly Lounge.*

No expense was spared to create The Ritz-Carlton, Millenia, Singapore's most lavish, modern hotel. It has an astonishing 4,200-piece modern art collection, which includes works by Frank Stella, Andy Warhol and Dale Chihuly; its breathtaking architecture is the product of Pritzker prize winner Kevin Roche.

The location and construction of The Ritz-Carlton, Millenia was done with the intent of providing spectacular views from every room. All guest rooms and bathrooms offer stunning panoramas of either Marina Bay or Kallang Bay and the city skyline. Each of the oversized rooms is also designed as a modern lap of luxury, featuring large marble-tiled bathrooms with octagonal windows, European bath amenities, high-speed Internet access, plush furniture and walk-in wardrobes.

At the top of The Ritz-Carlton, Millenia is the prestigious Ritz-Carlton Club, which comprises 128 club rooms that include 19 one-bedroom suites, 3 two-bedroom suites and The Ritz-Carlton Suite.

Guests of The Ritz-Carlton Club enjoy a dedicated concierge service, a private Club Lounge where complimentary culinary and beverage presentations are served, and even more luxurious rooms that have feather beds with fluffy goose down duvets, Bulgari bath amenities, flat-screen televisions, DVD players and personal butler service.

Food lovers will be spoilt for choice at The Ritz-Carlton, Millenia. The Summer Pavilion, which is set in a Suzhou rock garden, is the hotel's signature restaurant. It serves traditional Cantonese cuisine in a modern setting.

Greenhouse is the hotel's all-day restaurant, featuring food influenced by international cuisines. Seating a maximum of 240 guests, Greenhouse has built a name as Singapore's premier Sunday champagne brunch affair.

The Chihuly Lounge offers afternoon tea, while cocktails and champagne may be enjoyed throughout the day.

Conference facilities include the 1,094-sq m (11,781-sq ft) Grand Ballroom that features modern audio-visual and lighting equipment, the stylish Chihuly Room and 12 meeting and function rooms.

The fitness centre and spa is the perfect place to work out or unwind after a long day. The Spa boasts a unique Chocolate De-Ager treatment—a bath of warmed chocolate mixed with sweet almond oil—that uses the anti-aging properties of cocoa.

The Ritz-Carlton, Millenia provides one of the finest hotel experiences in Asia. It has developed a reputation for impeccable service and has won 'Best Accommodation Experience' from the Singapore Tourism Board, 'Best Hotel in Asia' from *Business Asia* and 'Best Business Hotel in Asia' from *Finance Asia*.

PHOTOGRAPHS COURTESY OF THE RITZ-CARLTON, MILLENIA SINGAPORE.

FACTS

ROOMS 608 rooms • 19 one-bedroom suites • 3 two-bedroom suites • 1 Ritz-Carlton suite
FOOD Summer Pavilion: Cantonese • Greenhouse: international
DRINK Chihuly Lounge • Pool Bar
FEATURES babysitting • gift shop • florist • fitness centre • spa • technology butler • limousine pickup • executive business services • high-speed Internet access • meeting rooms
NEARBY business and financial district • civic and cultural district • shopping • theatre • museums • entertainment • bars and clubs • dining • sightseeing • city tour
CONTACT 7 Raffles Avenue, Singapore 039799 • telephone: +65.6337 8888 • facsimile: +65.6338 0001 • email: rc.sinrz.reservations@ritzcarlton.com • website: www.ritzcarlton.com/hotels/singapore

Equinox Complex

THIS PAGE: *The floor-to-ceiling windows offer magnificent views of Singapore and distant shores while diners are pampered by personalised service from the chef and staff.*

OPPOSITE: *Located on Level 69, a suite of four private dining rooms complements Equinox Restaurant perfectly.*

Launched in 2001, Equinox Complex is one of Singapore's most exciting dining and entertainment venues and continues to attract and impress its many visitors. The expansive 3,700-sq m (40,000-sq ft) complex comprises five restaurants and bars, and a private dining room that seats over 900 people.

Equinox Complex's location is a huge draw in itself. Situated on levels 70 through 72 of Swissôtel The Stamford, it provides magnificent views of Singapore, Malaysia and Indonesia. Very few restaurants can boast such spectacular vistas of one country, much less of three.

The name Equinox is rooted in the ideals of perfection and balance. It refers to the time when day and night are of equal lengths, a phenomenon which only occurs on two days in a year. At the Complex, perfection and harmony are attainable throughout the whole year.

The memorable experience at Equinox begins on Level 1, where the ultra sleek

Very few restaurants can boast such spectacular vistas of one country, much less of three.

Introbar welcomes guests with an extensive aperitif selection, including the latest martinis, beers, wines and the house specialty—cocktails. All cocktails are individually mixed at the guests' tables by a team of bartenders. This special service has earned Introbar an unofficial title: it is also known as the Bartenders' Bar.

Upon entering Equinox Restaurant, many guests will find themselves rooted in awe at the head of the grand staircase which leads to the dining area. Three-storey-high teak and rice paper lanterns and Ming-inspired wooden trellises hang from the ceiling. On one side is a glowing floor-to-ceiling mother-of-pearl wall, and on the other, huge glass windows present a view of foreign lands beckoning from the horizon. The restaurant's two kitchens, which serve lunch, high tea and dinner, offer spectacular dishes to complement the magnificent view.

Seasonal modern French food is served at Jaan, which is defined by exciting colours and bold lines. The view of Singapore's waters is complemented by dazzling Murano wave crystals hanging from the restaurant's ceiling, evoking images of ocean waves breaking over a shoreline.

New Asia Bar is intriguingly unusual, with vibrant colours, unconventional furnishings and floors that tilt at a 20-degree angle. Day or night, it serves up bar food, drinks and contemporary music. When night falls, the in-house DJ takes over with a mix of modern groove, house and techno music.

For quiet after-dinner drinks, there is the club-like luxury of City Space, an intimate lounge perfect for a cigar or two accompanied by unobtrusive lounge music.

PHOTOGRAPHS COURTESY OF EQUINOX COMPLEX.

FACTS

SEATS	Introbar: 80 • Equinox Restaurant: 165 • Jaan: 60 • New Asia Bar: 180 • City Space: 53 • Equinox Private Dining: 10 to 400
FOOD	Equinox Restaurant: pure Asian or pure Western • Jaan: modern French
DRINK	New Asia Bar • Introbar • City Space
FEATURES	4 private dining rooms
NEARBY	Raffles City Shopping Centre • Chijmes • Esplanade – Theatres on the Bay • Suntec Singapore International Convention & Exhibition Centre
CONTACT	2 Stamford Road, Swissôtel The Stamford, Levels 1, 69–72, Singapore 178882 • telephone: +65 6837 3322 • facsimile: +65 6837 3222 • email: reservations@equinoxcomplex.com • website: www.equinoxcomplex.com

Flutes at the Fort

THIS PAGE (FROM TOP): *The historic black-and-white colonial bungalow tucked away from the city is a unique location for this exclusive restaurant; fine dining in a garden setting.*

OPPOSITE (FROM LEFT): *Healthy and fresh ingredients are featured prominently on the menu; peaceful surroundings coupled with a cosy interior make this restaurant a great place to hold parties.*

Located amongst the lush greenery of Fort Canning Park, this restaurant is housed in a quaint black-and-white 1908 colonial bungalow. This elegant and beautifully restored bungalow was once the home of various fire chiefs and their families when the British forces were installed at the historic Hill Street Fire Station located down the road.

Flutes at the Fort endeavours to create a vineyard-inspired experience for its diners, and in many ways, it has achieved its objective. The relaxed ambience, coupled with good service, food and wine, evokes the quietude and calm of vineyard restaurants around the world.

Tucked amidst verdant foliage on a small hill, the surrounding environment is refreshingly serene. Patrons who wish to escape the humidity are ushered into air-conditioned comfort, and into the cosy Fire Chief's Retreat, Court Room or Lewin Room, whilst those who enjoy nature, bird and insect calls can request to be seated at the large, wooden-deck veranda overlooking the lush and tranquil gardens.

The restaurant serves modern Australian cuisine, and the menu is packed with vibrant and light flavours, seasoned with the freshest of ingredients to provide healthy, delicious and memorable meals.

...the relaxed ambience...evokes the quietude and calm of vineyard restaurants...

Some of the chef's recommendations include starters like Seared West Australian Scallops, which comes with an interesting Asian twist—the dish is served with mushroom and soba noodle salad tossed in truffle soy dressing.

For the main course, the Roasted Grain-Fed Australian Lamb Rack and Pan-Seared Black Cod Fillet are favourites among regulars.

The restaurant also offers an extensive wine list, featuring the best of New and Old World wines. All the wines have been carefully selected by the chef to complement each item on the menu.

The Lewin Room, a glass-fronted room on the veranda, used to be the playroom of the fire chief's children. Named after Major General EO Lewin, who was commanding officer of the British forces in Singapore in the early 1930s, the room has since been converted into a wine cellar for the restaurant's collection of over 200 Australian wines, and a fine library filled with historical books about Singapore.

The Lewin Room also serves as a private dining and function room. The wooden floor, high ceiling and a large, square dining table provides a spacious yet cosy setting for parties of up to 16 people.

Flutes at the Fort's unique private rooms and exclusive location make it a great place to host celebratory events such as corporate functions, engagement parties, birthdays, wedding solemnisation and receptions.

FACTS

SEATS	110
FOOD	modern Australian • vegetarian options available • customised menus
DRINK	extensive wine list
FEATURES	Lewin Room for up to 16 people • private/corporate functions
NEARBY	Fort Canning Park • Singapore Philatelic Museum • Asian Civilisations Museum, Armenian Street • National Archives • Raffles City Shopping Centre
CONTACT	21 Lewin Terrace, Fort Canning Park, Singapore 179290 • telephone: +65.6338 8770 • facsimile: +65.6338 8780 • email: flutes@flutesatthefort.com.sg • website: www.flutesatthefort.com.sg

The Forbidden City by IndoChine

THIS PAGE: Impressive terracotta sculptures add the wow factor.

OPPOSITE: Chinese opulence in the dining area of Restaurant Madame Butterfly.

Step back in time at The Forbidden City, IndoChine's magnificent restaurant and bar along Clark Quay. The grand old riverhouse where the Forbidden City stands has been transformed into a palatial dining venue. Towering terracotta warriors greet guests at the entrance. The interiors exude both elegant antiquity and modern sophistication. Restaurant Madame Butterfly on the top floor and Bar CoCoon at the ground floor offer a unique gallery-cum-dining concept in the sprawling 6,706-m (22,000-sq ft) grounds, making The Forbidden City one of the largest galleries of Chinese paintings, artefacts and antiques in Southeast Asia.

Visual art goes hand in hand with culinary art at the Forbidden City, where Chinese cuisine gets an Indochinese twist.

Unlike other Chinese restaurants however, IndoChine founder Michael Ma has made it a policy not to serve certain foods such as sharks' fin, caviar and blue and yellow fin tuna at the Forbidden City as well as in his other 23 award-winning restaurants, bars, cafés and clubs. Instead, the menu features "nutriceutical" food, which emphasises the nutritional and pharmaceutical benefits of certain ingredients such as herbs and vegetables, and well-balanced meals that are high in fibre, essential minerals and taste.

As in the traditional style of Chinese houses, the upper floor has a view of the floor below. The open space in

Restaurant Madame Butterfly that is flanked by wooden railings is where one can look down to Bar CoCoon. Major events such as the Paris International Olympic Committee 2012 bid party and Cirque du Soleil's Quidam post-premiere party have been held in its unique interiors.

Chinese paintings, calligraphy and art from world-renowned artists adorn the restaurant walls while Ming vases, Tang antiques and Qing artefacts line the shelves, exalting 5,000 years of Chinese civilisation and culture—truly a feast for the eyes. The

traditional furniture and the cutlery are all handmade by Chinese master craftsmen, blurring the lines as to where the art gallery ends and the restaurant begins. Creativity can also be seen in the menu, which has ingeniously named dishes such as Imperial Banquet Chicken and Concubine's Delicacy.

Food choices range from crispy Summer Palace Duck wrapped in a pancake tortilla with celery, Cucumber and Sweet Black Sauce, succulent King Prawns with Lychee, to Sea Cucumber and Monkey Head Mushrooms for vegetarians. Restaurant Madame Butterfly breaks away

After a sumptuous dinner, lounge in Bar CoCoon's luxurious opium beds, enveloped by silk lanterns and drapery. Jasmine incense adds to the sensual eastern ambience of the bar. Some of the signature drinks at Bar CoCoon are the Terracota and Butterfly Effect. Vinto Terrino, which is also popular, was perfected by Michael Ma himself.

New Zealand's premium 42 Below Vodka chose Bar CoCoon to premiere its Ice Bar, which in Singapore goes by the name, The Ice Palace. The original Forbidden City in Beijing was rumored to have its own ice palace where the emperor sent his unwanted concubines. In Bar CoCoon, the Ice Palace has a different purpose—it is dedicated to the serving and drinking of vodka. The water used in 42 Below Vodka is sourced from beneath an extinct volcano. It sets the world benchmark for water purity, with an AA rating from the World Health Organisation.

The hand-sculpted bar is hosted in a structure measuring 5 by 4 m (16 by 13 ft). It is reinforced with triple-glazed safety glass with a nitric oxide system to minimise condensation and is designed to withstand extreme conditions.

The frozen interior—including the bar top, tables and vodka glasses—is constructed entirely from ice, while the

from the predictable with its Grilled Venison with Aromatic Herbs—venison fillet marinated with lemongrass, galangal, and kaffir lime leaves, which comes with a sour and spicy Vietnamese dip—and a drunken stir-fried ostrich that is also part of its menu. Its other offerings employ a broad spectrum of cooking methods that include stir frying, pan searing, baling and claypot cooking, with some dishes served on sizzling hot plates.

Titillate your tastebuds with desserts such as White Chocolate Oolong Tea—traditional oolong tea in a white chocolate bomb, and Romance of the Kingdom—glutinous rice balls with a golden ginger infusion, ginko nuts and young coconut flesh, served with sesame ice cream.

floor is tightly packed with snow. Guests are provided with fur jackets and gloves at the entrance, which is air-locked to maintain the sub-zero temperature inside.

Drinking at the Ice Palace is quite different from drinking in a normal bar. At –15°C, it is impossible to serve beverages like wine or beer. 42 Below's full-time mixologists are dedicated to concocting drinks that are especially for the intense cold. The trained bar staff are also at hand to monitor the guests, making sure that they don't overexpose themselves to the frigid temperature at the bar.

Accompanying the extensive drinks list is Bar CoCoon's menu of finger food. Lounge food includes chicken wings, deep fried spring rolls, fresh rice paper prawn rolls and fried fish with aromatic spicy sauce.

The intimate Ice Palace has seating for only 20 persons. As the latest alternative clubbing venue for the jet set, it is no doubt the coolest bar in Singapore.

PHOTOGRAPHS COURTESY OF THE FORBIDDEN CITY AND MING.

FACTS

SEATS	Restaurant Madame Butterfly: 180 • Bar CoCoon: 300
FOOD	contemporary Indochinese
DRINK	Old and New World wines • cocktails • liquor
FEATURES	wine cellar • bar • ice bar
NEARBY	Boat Quay • River Valley
CONTACT	The Forbidden City, 3A Merchant's Court #01-02, River Valley Road, Singapore 179020 • telephone: +65.6557 6266 (Restaurant Madame Butterfly) • telephone: +65.6557 6268 (Bar CoCoon) • facsimile: +65.6337 4358 • email: enquiry@indochine.com.sg • website: www.indochine.com.sg

Garibaldi Group of Restaurants

Garibaldi is located along Purvis Street, which is a stone's throw away from the historic Raffles Hotel. The superb cuisine and unsurpassed wine cellar of this stylish restaurant make it a favourite haunt of food and wine enthusiasts.

Authentic Italian dishes such as Steamed Lobster Marinated in Fresh Herbs and Homemade Tortellini Filled with Pumpkin bring flavours of the homeland to the table. There are two menus: the à la carte menu and the gourmet menu, which consists of five dishes. Among Garibaldi's specialties are Blue Swimmer Crab Salad with Avocado and Cherry Tomatoes, Angel Hair Pasta with Lobster and Braised Veal Shank with Saffron Risotto.

Chef Roberto Galetti concocts mouth-watering dishes with the freshest ingredients imported from Italy to maintain the taste and originality of the cuisine. Galetti, who has been in the business for more than twenty years, has headed some of the best Italian kitchens around the world. He relies purely on the best seasonal ingredients and works to present them in a way that best highlights their natural goodness.

Garibaldi has one of the largest collection of wines in Singapore, with over 300 labels. Its wine list includes some of Italy's best wines, a few of which are exclusive to the restaurant. Its bar offers a selection of exotic cocktails, and serves wines not only from Italy but also from France, Australia, California and other wine-making regions around the world.

Garibaldi has two other outlets: Menotti the Original Italian Café and Ricciotti Italian Deli and Pastry.

Menotti in Raffles City has a chocolate menu, which offers a selection of drinking

THIS PAGE (FROM LEFT): Garibaldi's comfortable interiors are perfect for casual social gatherings; Blue Swimmer Crab Salad with Avocado and Cherry Tomatoes and Angel Hair Pasta with Lobster.
OPPOSITE: The design for Menotti is stylish and energetic.

cru chocolates. Here, Michel Cluizel artisan chocolates—plantation crus that are the finest in the world—are melted and served with frothy milk on the side. Menotti has indoor and outdoor seating and has a warm, intimate ambience that is created by the use of natural materials like real leather, solid wood, marble and copper panels. Its modern interiors are further enhanced by the lighting design of Dr Luigi Tassoni from FLOS Italy.

As Singapore's most authentic Italian delicatessen, gourmet pastry shop and café, Ricciotti serves food that reflects true Italian tradition. It is located along the historic Singapore River and has a casual and welcoming atmosphere. Stefano Deiuri, one of Italy's top pastry chefs, whips up a mind boggling array of gourmet Italian pastries. Their delectable gelato is made in the original Sicilian style. Through its creative chefs, the Garibaldi group continues to cook up exciting new dishes that bring the authentic flavours of Italy in a relaxed, contemporary atmosphere.

PHOTOGRAPHS COURTESY OF GARIBALDI GROUP.

FACTS

SEATS	Garibaldi: 82 • Menotti: 90 • Ricciotti: 54
FOOD	authentic Italian
DRINK	extensive wine list • bar
FEATURES	Garibaldi: fresh imported ingredients • Menotti: chocolate menu •
NEARBY	Raffles City Shopping Centre • Chijmes • Raffles Hotel
CONTACT	Garibaldi Italian Restaurant + Bar, 36 Purvis Street #01-02 Singapore 188613 • telephone: +65.6837 1468 • Menotti The Original Italian Café, Raffles City Shopping Centre #01-17, North Bridge Road, Singapore 179103 • telephone: +65.6333 9366 • Ricciotti Italian Deli + Pastry, 20 Upper Circular Road, The Riverwalk #B1-49/50 Singapore 058416 • telephone: +65.6533 9060 • email: admin@garibaldi.com.sg • website: www.garibaldi.com.sg

IndoChine Waterfront Restaurant

The IndoChine Waterfront Restaurant along the Singapore River offers a unique juxtaposition of Old World charm and modern day chic. With one of the finest river vistas in Singapore, this world-class fine-dining establishment serves award-winning cuisine inspired by the flavours of Indochina.

The extensive menu presents authentic Cambodian, Vietnamese and Laotian dishes that are fresh, flavoursome and healthy. The fusion of Indochinese flavours with cosmopolitan cuisine is unique to the IndoChine Group and reflects its founder Michael Ma's childhood in Laos and upbringing in Australia. It also embodies his lifelong passion for good food, entertainment and design. The restaurant, which *Singapore Tatler* listed as one of the Best Restaurants in Singapore in 2004, shares the Empress Place building with the Asian Civilisations Museum. Its location alone speaks for the high regard given to the IndoChine Group's contribution to the culinary adventure, which is part of the exploration of Asian culture.

As is characteristic of Indochinese cuisine, fresh vegetables and herbs are used in abundance. There are no artificial flavourings, colourings and preservatives. The IndoChine House Salad, for example, contains no oil and requires great skill and accuracy to prepare in the traditional Laotian fashion. Other dishes such as the Laotian marinated chicken in lemon juice, Cambodian tiger prawns in holy basil and garlic sauce and French beef stew IndoChine style are all prepared with the health-conscious in mind.

IndoChine Waterfront's elaborate interiors make an unforgettable setting for social events and parties. Czechoslovakian crystal chandeliers in the shape of lotus flowers, towering Sukhothai Buddha statues, rare Shan antiques and the first

...Cambodian, Vietnamese and Laotian dishes that are fresh, flavoursome and healthy.

2005, the closing party of the International Olympics Committee was also held here. IndoChine Waterfront's bar, café and restaurant offer a gastronomic and visual feast that has made it a sought-after venue for glamorous corporate functions.

custom-made Ming Dynasty-style chairs made of stainless steel and leather are just some of its priceless conservation pieces.

The al fresco dining area at Siem Reap II is where one can enjoy Eastern and Western meals or afternoon tea. Bar Opiume, on the other hand, has been the preferred venue for world-class acts and corporate events such as the MTV Asia Awards post-award parties. In

FACTS

SEATS	IndoChine Waterfront: 390 • Bar Opiume: 320 • Siem Reap II: 175
FOOD	contemporary Indochinese
DRINK	Italian wines • Old and New World wines • cocktails
FEATURES	wine cellar • bar • artefacts
NEARBY	Fullerton Hotel • Esplanade – Theatres on the Bay • Singapore River • Boat Quay
CONTACT	1 Empress Place, Asian Civilisations Museum, Singapore 179555 • telephone: +65.6339 1720 (IndoChine Waterfront Restaurant), +65.6339 2876 (Bar Opiume), +65.6338 7596 (Siem Reap II) • facsimile: +65.6339 0420 • email: enquiry@indochine.com.sg • website: www.indochine.com.sg/empressplace.htm

PHOTOGRAPHS COURTESY OF INDOCHINE WATERFRONT RESTAURANT AND MING.

My Humble House

THIS PAGE (FROM LEFT): *My Humble House is known for contemporary Chinese cuisine, with creations like this; a sensuous table setting; a dining area one will remember for its décor as much as the food served in it; An illuminated column of crystal raindrops in the bar area.*

OPPOSITE: *The private dining room offers a view of chefs at work.*

Renowned for its poetic artistry in design, cuisine and service, My Humble House is the Tung Lok Group's first artistic restaurant, conceived to provide an experience that is captivating to both the palate and the eye.

Thespian dining chairs covered in suede and cowhide sit alongside traditional teak and rosewood furniture.

In the private dining room, guests are treated to a performance of a culinary kind. On a stage of pure white marble overlooking the open kitchen, diners watch as chefs create their magic. Specially designed by Kuro Mende, one of the world's best lighting specialists, the restaurant has three different mood lightings which change according to the time of day.

As Director of Kitchens for Tung Lok Restaurants, Sam Leong has won numerous accolades for his mastery in the kitchen, including his hat trick win of the prestigious World Gourmet Summit Awards of Excellence for 'Asian Ethnic Chef of the Year' in 2001, 2002 and 2004, as well as 'Chef of the Year' and 'Executive Chef of the Year' in 2005.

...poetic artistry in design, cuisine and service...

The menu reads like classical Chinese literature, with poetic descriptions such as Dancing With The Wind—Braised Shark's Fin with Seafood Consommé served in Young Coconut, and Blooms in Silent Shadow—Oven-baked Rack of Lamb in Balsamic Port Wine with Asparagus. This poetic theme further translates itself on the plate where traditional and progressive Chinese cuisine is transformed into modern artistry.

Located in Esplanade Mall within Singapore's landmark national performing arts centre, Esplanade – Theatres on the Bay, the restaurant is ideally situated against the scenic backdrop of Marina Bay. In August 2003, My Humble House was recognised as one of the 'Top 10 Romantic Spots in Singapore' in 2003 and was also awarded 'Asian Ethnic Restaurant of the Year' at the World Gourmet Summit Awards of Excellence in 2006. With the creativity it puts into the cuisine and its presentation, My Humble House gives new meaning to the art of dining.

FACTS

SEATS	110 • private dining room: 12
FOOD	contemporary Chinese
DRINK	a wide variety of wines • champagne and cocktails
FEATURES	private dining room • main dining area with waterfront view
NEARBY	Marina Square • Raffles City Shopping Centre • civic district
CONTACT	8 Raffles Avenue, #02-27/29 Esplanade Mall, Singapore 039802 • telephone: +65.6423 1881 • facsimile: +65.6423 1551 • email: myhumblehouse@tunglok.com • website: www.tunglok.com

PHOTOGRAPHS COURTESY OF MY HUMBLE HOUSE.

Pierside Kitchen + Bar and Toast

Pierside kitchen&bar is a short walk from the business district and three landmarks: The Fullerton Hotel, Esplanade – Theatres on the Bay and the Merlion statue at the marina. Its proximity to these areas give pierside its fair share of tourists. Its usual clients however, are business executives and theatre-goers.

Seafood dominates the menu at pierside. Executive Chef Robin Ho, who intimates that food is like fashion, constantly introduces new creations. The modern international cuisine offered here uses ingredients sourced from all over the world and employs a predominantly French style of cooking. Oven-Roasted Miso Cod, New Potatoes and Sweet Peas; Braised Lamb Shank and Oriental Spices; Snapper Pie, Smoked Tomato and White Truffle Oil;

Hazelnut-Crusted King Prawns, Lemongrass and Lobster Sauce; and Arugula Pappardelle, Braised Oxtail and Horseradish are mainstays in the menu. Plateau de Fruits de Mer, a two-tiered seafood platter consisting of hot or deep-fried items on top and raw or cold items at the bottom, is also popular among diners. The Sommelier's Table, a set menu consisting of four courses each paired with a different type of wine, is changed monthly.

The use of choice products is also evident in the quality of the drinks offered at the bar. Specialty drinks—the Cosmopolitan, Lychee Lemongrass Martini, and Grand Mimosa—as well as the other alcoholic beverages in the drinks list all use premium liquor. Pierside uses more than the usual amount to match the taste

THIS PAGE (FROM TOP): The subtle hues and lighting of pierside kitchen&bar's indoor dining area create a perfect backdrop for a romantic candlelit dinner; seafood is the highlight at pierside kitchen&bar, which is famous for its rockfish. OPPOSITE: Power breakfast selections from Toast, which also carries signature home-baked cakes and pastries from the Marmalade Pantry.

At OUB Centre in the heart of the business district is Toast, a café that distinguishes itself through the gourmet ingredients and market fresh produce it uses for its soups, salads and sandwiches. Toast's products are either homemade or freshly prepared. Signature items are the Masala Chicken Wrap, Roast Beef, Avocado Caesar Wrap, Kaya Toasties and Peanut Butter and Banana Toasties. It also gives local food a twist: its Kaya Toasties, for instance, use panini instead of toasted bread. Served in substantial portions, these meals provide a nutritious and filling alternative to regular coffeeshop fare.

Toast is a popular lunch choice for busy professionals and the health-conscious. Apart from lunches, Toast offers power breakfasts, vegetarian selections and food for tea breaks. It also carries Marmalade Pantry's most popular cakes and home-baked cupcakes— delicious desserts that the Marmalade Group has become known for. Toast has another outlet at Ngee Ann City in Orchard Road.

Pierside kitchen&bar and Toast belong to the Marmalade Group, which also owns Marmalade Pantry in Orchard Road. Its savouries, pastries and cakes have made it very popular choice for weekend brunch.

Marmalade at Home, the group's catering arm, offers services for different events, from intimate dinner parties to grand celebrations.

of its guests, 80% of whom are expatriates. Waterfront dining is one of the restaurant's main attractions. The eight seats right next to the water are always in demand.

The al fresco bar offers the best view of fireworks displays during festivities like New Year's Eve and National Day. Recently renovated to accommodate larger events, the bar offers tapas, cocktails, and champagne. The view of passing bumboats and city lights complete the backdrop to a perfect evening.

FACTS		
SEATS	pierside kitchen&bar indoor dining area: 75, al fresco and bar area: 120 • Toast OUB Centre: 40	
FOOD	pierside kitchen&bar: modern international • Toast: sandwiches and pastries	
DRINK	wine cellar • bar	
FEATURES	pierside kitchen&bar: waterfront dining • Toast: gourmet café	
NEARBY	Raffles Place • Esplanade – Theatres on the Bay • The Arts House • Boat Quay	
CONTACT	pierside kitchen&bar: #01-01 One Fullerton, Singapore 049214 • Toast 1 Raffles Place, #01-09 OUB Centre, Singapore 048616 • telephone: +65.6438 0400 (pierside kitchen&bar), 165.6534 1755 (Toast) • facsimile: +65.6438 3436 (pierside kitchen&bar), +65.6534 1756 (Toast) • website: www.marmaladegroup.com	

PHOTOGRAPHS COURTESY OF THE MARMALADE GROUP.

Rang Mahal

Rang Mahal fine dining Indian restaurant has been serving up authentic menus drawn from the richness and abundance of India's heritage since 1971. Located on Level 3 of Pan Pacific Singapore, a visit to the restaurant is a treat for all the senses. Soothing colours, artful décor and delicious aromas work together to heighten the consciousness to the world-class food, ambience and service, gently swaying drapes and delicately carved figurines.

Natural elements like granite, limestone and dark wood dominate the interiors of Rang Mahal, conjuring images of an exotic India. Granite works by the celebrated sculptor Satish Gujral adorn the restaurant, as do specially commissioned madhubani paintings—created using vegetable dyes on hand-made paper—by Chandra Bhushan. These artworks, which bear religious motifs and icons, offer an interesting insight into the artistic cultures of India.

Rang Mahal's array of delectable dishes is inspired by the cuisines of the northern, southern and coastal regions of India. Traditional recipes are given a modern twist in presentation and taste, all beautifully recreated by a team of chefs hand-picked for their creativity and passion. With the trend towards healthy living, alternative ingredients and oils have also been integrated into the recipes.

At the restaurant's Bread Bar is the popular herb naan, which is made with garlic, tulsi and cumin.

The restaurant also offers special menus for vegetarians, as well as dishes that cater to diners from the Jain society, a Hindu sect that abstains from consuming organic roots.

THIS PAGE (FROM TOP): The restaurant offers a menu filled with authentic Indian specialty dishes and sweets; the modern décor is accented with classical Indian art.

OPPOSITE: The dining room is marked by earthy shades, sleek furnishing and plush carpeting.

As befitting royalty—a status accorded to each diner—every item from the menu is freshly made using only the finest gourmet ingredients, all specially flown in from India. To accompany the delectable dishes is a selection of over 150 labels and vintages from the restaurant's cellar.

The restaurant's signature dishes include tandoori oyster, marinated in spices and grilled to perfection in a tandoor.

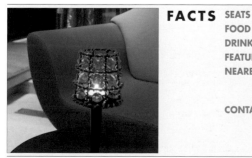

PHOTOGRAPHS COURTESY OF RANG MAHAL.

FACTS	**SEATS**	dining hall: 120 • private room: 20 • lounge: 8
	FOOD	refined Indian • vegetarian options available
	DRINK	extensive wine list
	FEATURES	personal butler service for private rooms • catering service
	NEARBY	Raffles City Shopping Centre • Chijmes • CityLink Mall • Millennia Walk • Suntec Singapore International Convention & Exhibition Centre • Esplanade – Theatres on the Bay • Marina Square Shopping Centre
	CONTACT	Rang Mahal, Pan Pacific Singapore, Level 3, 7 Raffles Boulevard, Marina Square, Singapore 039595 • telephone: +65.6333 1788 • facsimile: +65.6333 1660 • email: rangmahal@hind.com.sg • website: www.rangmahal.com.sg

Saint Julien Le Restaurant

THIS PAGE (FROM TOP): *The well-lit dining area has a view of the central business district and Esplanade – Theatres on the Bay; classic cuisine as it was enjoyed by the French upper class of an older generation.*

OPPOSITE: *Saint Julien glows like a beacon at the edge of the river.*

Its location already sparks interest: Saint Julien Le Restaurant is in The Fullerton Waterboat House, which has a view of the Singapore skyline and Esplanade – Theatres on the Bay. The day and nighttime views from this historical building, which once supplied water to ships offshore, provide a backdrop to this venue for fine French cuisine.

Awarded 'Best Restaurant of the Year 2006' by the World Gourmet Summit and the Singapore Tourism Board, Saint Julien is run by the husband and wife team of Julien Bompard and Edith Lai. It offers dishes such as Terrine of Foie Gras with Spices, Honey, and Sweet and Sour Shallots; Lobster Bisque Soup with Sea Scallop, Garlic Aioli and Croutons; Roasted Codfish à la Provençal with Caramelised Balsamic Vinegar and Basil Oil; and Seared Challand Duck Suprème with Mushroom Sauce and Potato Confit. The cooking style Chef Bompard uses to create them is greatly influenced by his Burgundy and Provençal heritage. There are four menus, among which are the seven-course Menu Saint Julien and the à la carte menu, which has a selection of French cheese and vegetarian dishes. A special menu is prepared

for guests in the private dining room. To complement the meal are selections from a comprehensive wine list: vintages from France and prominent New World wines from Australia and New Zealand.

Chef Bompard honed his culinary skills under renowned chefs Alain Dutournier, Louis Outhier at the L'Oasis on the Côte d'Azur, and the three-star Michelin chef Jacques Lameloise. He has lent his expertise to French restaurants Le Normandie in Bangkok and Gaddi's in Hong Kong. He has two five-star Diamond Awards as "One of the Best Chefs in the World" from the American Academy Hospitality Sciences and was also named 'Global Chef of the Year 2006' by at-sunrise Culinary Academy, Singapore.

Edith Lai, who has spent years working in hotels around the world, gives a personal touch to Saint Julien and makes guests feel at home. She was recognised as 'Best Restaurant Manager of the Year' for 2005 by the World Gourmet Summit Awards of Excellence.

PHOTOGRAPHS COURTESY OF SAINT JULIEN LE RESTAURANT.

FACTS

SEATS	main dining room: 70 • room for couples: 2 • private room: 14
FOOD	traditional French
DRINK	wine list
FEATURES	set lunch and dinner menus • à la carte menu • exclusive room for couples • complimentary valet parking
NEARBY	Raffles Place • The Arts House • Esplanade – Theatres by the Bay • One Fullerton • central business district
CONTACT	3 Fullerton Road, #02-01 The Fullerton Waterboat House, Singapore 049215 • telephone: +65.6534 5947 • facsimile: +65.6534 5949 • email: info@saintjulien.com.sg • website: www.saintjulien.com.sg

Saint Pierre The Restaurant

Saint Pierre is a 70-seater restaurant serving innovative French cuisine. It first opened in December 2000. Owner and executive chef Emmanuel Stroobant trained in some of the best restaurants in Belgium, which included Michelin-starred establishments, before he came to Singapore to set up Saint Pierre. His dedication and culinary talents have earned him recognition from the Wine & Dine Awards and the World Gourmet Summit. He received awards for 'Most Innovative Menu', and 'Chef of the Year'. Both groups also named Saint Pierre 'Best New Restaurant' in 2002 and 2003.

Located in Central Mall near bustling entertainment areas like Clarke Quay, Boat Quay and Robertson Quay, Saint Pierre has gone a long way from its humble beginnings. Two private rooms with collapsible walls can accommodate 12 to 30 persons and are ideal for large parties. There is one more private room in the wine cellar that can take 10–14 persons.

THIS PAGE: *In this subtly-lit cosy dining room, the spotlight is on the food.*

OPPOSITE: *Elegant plating that also reflects the chef's playfulness and creativity.*

The dining area accommodates 40 persons, a number that Chef Stroobant finds comfortable to work with so that he can maintain the quality of the food, ambience and personalised service that have become Saint Pierre's trademarks.

Chef Stroobant's creativity is evident in his many variations for preparing escargot, foie gras and duck—regular stars in every French menu. His innovation can be seen in seafood dishes, where lobster, salmon, scallops, cod, crab and tuna are used. Specialties include Pan-Fried Foie Gras with Caramelised Green Apples and Old Port Wine Sauce, and Miso Marinated Braised Black Cod. Diners will find that the descriptions in the menu do justice to what they can expect on the table. Just as tempting are the list of desserts, which features favourites like crème brûlée and Grandma Stroobant's Flourless Belgian Chocolate Cake. There are always new dishes to look forward to because Chef Stroobant comes up with a new menu every three months. He also has special menus for occasions like Christmas Eve, New Year's Eve and Valentine's Day. Guests at Saint Pierre can enjoy French cuisine without enduring the stuffy ambience typically found in similar establishments.

Reservations are encouraged. Saint Pierre opens for lunch and dinner from Mondays to Fridays. It is open only for dinner on Saturdays.

FACTS		
SEATS	40 • Private rooms: 14–20, combined space for 36	
FOOD	contemporary French	
DRINK	extensive wine list	
FEATURES	2-course set lunch • 3-course set lunch • 4-course set lunch • à la carte and other set menus	
NEARBY	Clarke Quay • Boat Quay • Robertson Quay • river boat tours	
CONTACT	3 Magazine Road #01-01 Central Mall, Singapore 059570 • telephone: +65.6438 0887 • facsimile: +65.6438 4887 • email: edina@saintpierre.com.sg • website: www.saintpierre.com.sg	

San Marco The Restaurant

San Marco's kitchen is helmed by Stroobant's protégé Chef Kelvin Lee, who began his apprenticeship in Italian cuisine. He later joined Stroobant in the early days of his career and continued to hone his culinary skills at the Raffles Grill and later the Michelin-starred Jardin des Sens in Montpellier, France.

A glance at the menu shows staples of Italian cuisine such as risotto and homemade pasta featured along with dishes using duck, pigeon, foie gras and even suckling pig, which happens to be the house specialty.

San Marco also offers a 10-course degustation menu, which shows a French influence in Lee's Italian creations. Each dish is paired with a different type of wine.

Some of the dishes that should not be missed are Roasted Scallops on Fleur de Sel with Pine Nut-Olive Salsa, Homemade

Located in the former Lighthouse of Singapore, San Marco is a fine dining restaurant specialising in Northern Italian cuisine. Named after the Basilica in Venice, it is accessible through the eighth floor of the Fullerton Hotel.

San Marco is the brainchild of accomplished pastry chef Roxan Villareal and the husband and wife team of Edina Hong and award-winning chef Emmanuel Stroobant, the couple behind the popular restaurant Saint Pierre.

THIS PAGE (FROM TOP): The restaurant's dining room offers a panoramic view of the city; desserts, like the rest of the meal, evoke the chef's playfulness and creativity.

OPPOSITE: The black and white theme of the interiors provide a striking contrast to the vivid colours of the food at the table.

...a French influence in Lee's Italian creations.

Tomato Oil with Aged Aceto Balsamico and Crispy Basil Leaf; Homemade Fine de Claire Oyster Ravioli with Shallot Confit, Sun-dried Tomatoes, Wild Basil, Steamed Fava Beans with Tomato Concassee and Champagne Vinegar; Roasted Crispy Rack of Kurabuta Piglet with Caramelised Belly, Braised Loin, Broad Beans, Pepper Confetti and Arugula tossed with Homemade Apple Vinegar.

Desserts bear the talented touch of pastry chef and part owner Roxan Villareal. Apart from lending a hand in creating desserts, he also attends to guests during the entire duration of their meal.

San Marco is open for lunch and dinner from Mondays to Fridays. It is open for dinner on Saturdays and is closed on Sundays. Apart from the main dining area, there are two private rooms at the back that can each host six persons. The rooms can be joined to accommodate 14 persons. Reservations are encouraged.

FACTS		
SEATS	50 • 2 private rooms: 6 per room, combined space: 14
FOOD	contemporary Italian
DRINK	wine cellar
FEATURES	3-course set lunch • 5-course business set lunch • 10-course degustation menu
NEARBY	One Fullerton • central business district • Esplanade – Theatres on the Bay • Asian Civilisations Museum • Boat Quay • The Arts House
CONTACT	1 Fullerton Square, #08-00 The Fullerton Singapore, Singapore 049178 • telephone: +65.6438 4404 • facsimile: +65.6438 4424 • email: info@sanmarco.com.sg • website: www.sanmarco.com.sg

PHOTOGRAPHS COURTESY OF SAN MARCO THE RESTAURANT.

Zambuca Italian Restaurant + Bar

Zambuca offers contemporary Italian cuisine in a sleek, elegant setting. Located at the third level of the Pan Pacific Singapore, its rich materials, glass and ebony wood elements, dark teakwood floors and soft lighting combine to create an intimate, sophisticated ambience.

This award-winning restaurant is the latest in the highly successful Michelangelo's restaurant group. The 914-sq m (3,000-sq ft) dining room can seat up to 100 persons. Its al fresco dining area, which has a view of the main dining room and the towers of the Suntec City commercial centre can accommodate 110 persons.

Executive chef Dennis Sim has teamed with the group's culinary director Angelo Sanelli to create what has been described as an avant-garde menu. It features original seafood and classic game dishes—the modern mixed with traditional elements. Zambuca's specialties include Pan-fried Prawns with Fettucini, Tossed with Tomatoes, Capsicum, Artichoke and Spinach

THIS PAGE: Zambuca is the only dining establishment of the Michelangelo restaurant group that is located within a hotel.

OPPOSITE (FROM TOP): Warm lighting and ample seating at the bar; Desserts that are pleasing to the eye as well as the palate.

seminars, product launches, conferences and other functions. Likewise, the bar, dining room, wine cellar and al fresco areas can be integrated or isolated depending upon the needs of clients.

Cooking classes by Zambuca are available at Bentfork Cooking School at Blk 43 #01-64 Jalan Merah Saga, Chip Bee Gardens, Singapore 278115.

in Cream Sauce; and Penne Alla Siciliana with Spicy Italian Sausage, Olives, Tomatoes, Artichokes, Spinach and Thyme in a Homemade Tomato Sauce.

For wine connoisseurs, Zambuca also boasts a superb collection with more than 2,300 labels from France, Italy, Australia and the Americas. The restaurant won *Wine Spectator Magazine's* award of excellence from 2004 onwards, for having one of the most outstanding restaurant wine lists in the world. Its glass-walled wine cellar houses over 8,000 bottles. It also doubles as a private dining room for up to 12 persons.

Zambuca's bar features cool jazz and lounge music in the pre-dinner hours, and moves on to more contemporary artists as the evening progresses. The 396-sq m (1,300-sq ft) bar area can accommodate 25 people seated and 75 standing.

The establishment's various spaces can be maximised to cater to corporate events,

FACTS	**SEATS**	dining area: 100 • bar: 100 • wine cellar: 12 • al fresco area: 110
	FOOD	contemporary Italian
	DRINK	Extensive wine list • cocktails
	FEATURES	bar • al fresco area • glass-walled wine cellar which doubles as a private dining room
	NEARBY	Suntec Singapore International Convention & Exhibition Centre • Marina Square Shopping Centre • Millennia Walk • Esplanade – Theatres on the Bay
	CONTACT	7 Raffles Boulevard, #03-00 Pan Pacific Singapore, Singapore 039595 • telephone: +65.6337 8086 (Zambuca), +65.6475 4961 (Bentfork Cooking School) • facsimile: +65.6336 8494 • email: reservations@zambuca.com.sg, info@bentfork.sg • websites: www.zambuca.com.sg, www.bentfork.sg

PHOTOGRAPHS COURTESY OF ZAMBUCA ITALIAN RESTAURANT + BAR.

Felt

Felt is a multi-label boutique that caters to the modern woman with a sophisticated sense of fashion and individual style. The shop was conceptualised by owner Trixie Ong, who turned her love for Australian fashion into a thriving business.

Felt opened in 2004 and has since acquired a loyal fan base. Naturally, it is known for its Australian labels—which count among them Tina Kalivas, Paablo Nevada, Jayson Brunsdon and Lisa Ho. Felt also carries niche cult brands—from New Zealand designers Laurie Foon and Zambesi, to hot new UK designer Amr—and shoes from the iconic Eley Kishimoto. Other prestigious labels available at the shop are Astrophytum, Vince Maloney Retrospective, Georgiadis, Penelope Durston, Catherine Manuell Design, Ch3mical Three, Sophie Williams and Irina Volkonskii.

Offering an alternative to these international labels are collections sourced

THIS PAGE (FROM TOP): Fashion from Hansel by Jo Soh; hanging mannequins on the runway provide the illusion of models in suspended animation.

OPPOSITE (FROM LEFT): Jayson Brunsdon and Lisa Ho.

from the local design industry featuring Hansel by Jo Soh, which has been stirring interest in the local fashion scene as well as in Tokyo and Australia. New label Melly by Melly Mak takes off from the idea that a woman, just like a character in a movie, should be outfitted according to the roles she plays. Mak's passion for fashion, literature and old movies is evident in her work, showcasing wearable pieces with a thematic costume element. Her designs for Mime and song+kelly21 have appeared in shows in Singapore, Seoul and Sydney.

At Felt, shopping is more than just looking for the perfect outfit. Aesthetics become key in ensuring a thoroughly pleasurable experience for all visitors. The interiors are specially designed to evoke the couture ambience, truly befitting of the labels found at Felt. Ladies can sashay across the shop's runway not only so they can get a feel of the pieces they have on, but also to entertain their fantasy of being real-life catwalk models. With

highly selective buying practices, shoppers can rest assured that all pieces available at the shop are of fashion's finest. These elements collectively come together in creating a singular shopping experience at Felt.

To answer customers' call for unique evening wear, Felt recently added specially commissioned cocktail dresses by respected designers to its collection. These are adapted

from designs that just hit the fashion runways, so that one can have the latest look of the season without the hassle of having to wait.

Felt is committed to sourcing for the latest designs that are cutting-edge but also wearable. From corporate work wear to dressy outfits and glamorous evening dresses, the wide array of designer wear available meets the needs of any clotheshorse.

FACTS

PRODUCTS	women's fashion • fashion accessories
FEATURES	Australian, New Zealand and UK labels
NEARBY	St Andrew's Cathedral • Raffles City Shopping Centre • Chijmes • Raffles Hotel
CONTACT	11 Stamford Road, #01-18 Capitol Building, Singapore 178884 • telephone: +65 6837 3393 • facsimile: +65 6837 2837 • email: enquires@felt.com.sg • website: www.felt.com.sg

PHOTOGRAPHS COURTESY OF FELT.

Mod.Living

With its contemporary, chic and luxurious home furniture and furnishings, Mod.Living is a name synonymous with prestige and flair when it comes to designer furniture and home styling. Housed in an eye-catching two-storey gallery at the podium of Odeon Towers, the expansive space is home to a cache of the best Italian designs, including Molteni & C, Dada, Moroso, Antonio Lupi, Frighetto, Nube, Emmemobili, Artifort, Arflex, Misuraemme, Bravo and Tecmo.

Great design must be showcased in a tastefully designed space, and that is the reason Mod.Living is the first in the region to engage an Italian art director to style its

huge 920-sq m (10,000-sq ft) showroom. Lofty and airy, the gallery stands out by encompassing trend, art and culture in the presentation of its products.

The renowned Molteni & C is a brand exclusive to the gallery. In 2005, Molteni & C won the prestigious 'red dot: best of the best' award for its Diamond Tables. These tables have unusual legs, which appear to be twisted into themselves. The resulting design gives the tables a diamond-cut look. Created by Patricia Urquiola, the series is made up of intriguing and visually stunning pieces that will indubitably jazz up any home.

Shoppers are encouraged to find their own personalities through the collection of designer pieces available in this showroom.

For those who need some inspiration, they can glean innovative ideas from a fully furnished model apartment within the gallery. The model apartment is styled using furniture pieces from various brands, coupled with suitable lighting and home accessories for a finished look. Shoppers are encouraged to make frequent visits, as the styling consultants regularly change the displays and use this space to introduce new trends and interior concepts.

Home owners looking for fresh ideas and quality interiors will find a host of choices here. The in-house consultants are more than happy to recommend single signature pieces or thematic ensembles that work toward a Zen, futuristic, retro or even urban chic look. They also suggest how different pieces can be put together to create a style that suits each client's distinctive taste.

For those looking for more personalised advice and assistance, there's Mod.Living Home Styling, a value-added service where a home owner picks his favourite designer ensemble, and the consultants will do the rest. A home layout incorporating the ensemble and a mood board to complement the colour theme will be prepared upon consultation.

THIS PAGE: The kitchen and dining showroom's designer furniture and furnishings are just some of the stylish accessories you can bring to your own home.

OPPOSITE (FROM TOP): Mod.Living occupies the second storey of Odeon Towers. Its eye-catching sign is hard-to-miss; the gallery incorporates a model apartment complete with designer furniture and lighting.

FACTS

PRODUCTS	luxury designer furniture • home accessories • kitchen ensembles • bathroom ensembles • lightings • cabinets and wardrobes
FEATURES	home-styling service • model apartment
NEARBY	Raffles City Shopping Centre • Chijmes • CityLink Mall • Millennia Walk • Suntec Singapore International Convention & Exhibition Centre • Esplanade – Theatres on the Bay • Marina Square Shopping Centre
CONTACT	331 North Bridge Road, #02-01/08 Odeon Towers, Singapore 188720 • telephone: +65.6336 2286 • facsimile: +65 6352 7249 • email. enquiries@modliving.com.sg • website. www.modliving.com.sg

PHOTOGRAPHS COURTESY OF MOD.LIVING.

chinatown+
arabstreet+littleindia

Little India

Arab Street

Kallang Basin

Marina Bay

> Beaujolais Wine Bar
> Vanilla Home
> W Wine Bar
> Senso Ristorante + Bar
> Bar SáVanh + IndoChine Club Street
> Hotel 1929
> The Scarlet
> Oso Ristorante

Chinatown

Balestier Rd

Lavender St

Race Course Rd

Chander Rd

Serangoon Rd

Desker Rd

Kitchener Rd

Jalan Besar

Bukit Timah Rd

Rochor Canal Rd

Dunlop St

Sungei Rd

Rochor Canal Rd

Arab St

North Bridge Rd

Jalan Sultan

Ophir Rd

Baghdad

Beach Rd

Nicoll Highway

Selegie Rd

Middle Rd

Rochor Rd

Victoria St

Penang Rd

ley Rd

Bras Basah Rd

Stamford Rd

East Coast Parkway

Clemenceau Ave

Singapore River

Esplanade Drive

Rd

Rd

New Bridge Rd

Eu Tong Sen Rd

South Bridge Rd

Pickering St

Cross St

Club St

Keong Saik Rd

Neil Rd

Erskine

Amoy St

Telok Ayer St

Cecil St

Maxwell Rd

Robinson Rd

Shenton Way

Tanjong Pagar Rd

Cantonment Rd

ah Expressway

ethnic communities

In 1822, only a few years after he founded Singapore, Sir Stamford Raffles saw the need to draw up a detailed city plan to ensure the orderliness of the colony's growth. The plan included a layout of the zones for the major ethnic groups—the Chinese, the Malays and the Indians.

While the races today are no longer confined to geographical zones—these days the various ethnic groups live side by side all over the island—Chinatown, Little India and Arab Street still preserve the architecture of old shophouses and character that distinguished their respective communities.

chinatown

Chinatown covers a large area, stretching on either side of South Bridge Road, from North Canal Road to Cantonment Road. Since it is adjacent to the financial district, parts of Chinatown have become a beautiful blend of the old and the new, and of east and west. Skyscrapers and office buildings stand amid restored shophouses, many of which are occupied by restaurants and design firms.

The most popular and touristy part of Chinatown is a small area bounded by New Bridge and South Bridge roads on the west and east, and Upper Cross Street and Sago Lane on the north and south. Smith, Temple and Pagoda Streets offer excellent examples of baroque-style shophouses favoured by the Peranakans or Straits Chinese, and excellent shopping. There are many good places here to buy souvenirs, Chinese antiques and reproductions, porcelain, clothes and art.

Smith Street is also worth visitng at night; the Singapore Tourism Board has transformed it into what it calls a historic "food street". Come sundown, the road is closed off to traffic, and hawker stalls are allowed to set up on it. Tables and chairs fill the street and locals and tourists alike get a chance to experience eating out the old-fashioned way. Across South Bridge Road, Club Street and Ann Siang Hill demarcate a part of Chinatown that is relatively more modern. The Scarlet, one of the newest boutique hotels, is located here,

PAGE 160: *Chinese lanterns casting a subtle glow against strings of coloured lights.*

THIS PAGE: *Street hawkers selling 'ba kwa', a popular Chinese New Year snack, in Chinatown.*

OPPOSITE: *Chinatown is bustling with activity at night, especially during festive seasons.*

THIS PAGE (CLOCKWISE FROM TOP): Old photos and street signs at a bric-a-brac shop in Chinatown; stylish accomodation at Hotel 1929; a peek into the kitchen of the Majestic restaurant.
OPPOSITE: The red dot design museum holds exhibitions on product, communication and interior design.

as are lifestyle shops carrying Dean & DeLuca gourmet products, Scandinavian furniture, children's accessories from France, and Puma's high-end fashion and shoe lines. In between these shops is a mix of other establishments: upscale restaurants and bars, and a yoga studio.

Opposite The Scarlet, separated by a small public car park, is one of the city's most popular hawker centres. The Maxwell Food Centre lays claim to some of the best street food in town. One of the most popular stalls here that commands long lines is the "Hum Chim Peng" stall, which serves sweet and savoury traditional fried dough snacks. Loyal patrons form long queues not just because of the quality of food, but also because of the stall's unique, do-it-yourself policy. Customers are required to fry their own orders—a memorable if often sweaty experience. Around the corner, what used to be the Traffic Police's headquarters has been transformed into a design museum. This red building will house offices from the creative industry and restaurants and shops.

Another trendy area is Keong Saik Road, which in the past was known only for its seedy establishments. Now it has a champagne bar, a yoga studio and a chic vegetarian restaurant that is visited by some of the city's socialites. Hotel 1929, home to the popular restaurant, Ember, is also located here. Hotel 1929's owner recently opened the New Majestic Hotel and the Majestic restaurant one street away on Bukit Pasoh Road. A stunning old Chinese building was lovingly restored and transformed into this hip, new hideaway.

Tanjong Pagar and Neil Road south of South Bridge Road are lined with colourful, restored shophouses occupied by various cafés and restaurants. Qun Zhong Eating House at 21 Neil Road is well-known for its fried and boiled Beijing-style dumplings. Buko Nero, another cult restaurant in Tanjong Pagar Road, is owned and run by a husband and wife team, Oscar and Tracy Pasinato. Oscar, an Italian immigrant, is the chef who makes Buko Nero's Italian-Asian cuisine while his wife serves the guests. Despite being (or maybe because it is) very inexpensive, a table at Buko Nero may be the hardest reservation to get. At times, there is a two-month waiting list for their few small tables.

...what used to be the Traffic Police's headquarters has been transformed into a design museum.

Unlike other Chinatowns around the world, Singapore's Chinatown not only has Buddhist and Confucian places of worship, but also mosques and Hindu temples. Especially worth visiting are Thian Hock Keng, the oldest Chinese temple in the country, on Telok Ayer Street; and Sri Mariamman, a Hindu temple on South Bridge Road that is easily identifiable by the high tower at the entrance that is crowned by 72 deities.

This area of commerce also has small pockets of culture. Utterly Art in South Bridge Road and Art Seasons in Gemmill Lane are commercial galleries that specialise in local contemporary art. The largest and most important music groups are located near Chinatown as well: the Singapore Chinese Orchestra is the country's only professional Chinese orchestra. Consisting of 70 members, it has not only brought Chinese orchestral music to a wider audience in Singapore but also to those overseas. In 2005, it embarked on its very first European concert tour to places such as Budapest, London and Newcastle.

little india

The area occupied by Little India is a long, narrow stretch centred along Serangoon Road, spanning Bukit Timah Road and Balestier Road. While the majority of the country's Indian population is now spread across the island, Little India remains its cultural and commercial heart. It is a fantastic and colourful place to explore, especially during the weekends, and is still one of the top tourist destinations in Singapore.

Start with a visit to Tekka market at the corner of Serangoon Road and Bukit Timah Road. This multi-story building has one of the most popular food markets. There is an excellent hawker centre on the ground floor and several shops upstairs. Apart from Indian cafés and restaurants, there are sari shops, jewellery boutiques, Indian astrologists and stores selling a variety of goods such as spices, bangles, the latest soundtracks and DVDs of top Bollywood films. There are also several stores

THIS PAGE (FROM LEFT): *Thian Hock Keng is the oldest Chinese temple in Singapore; Hindi gods at the tower of the Sri Mariamman Temple.*

OPPOSITE (FROM TOP): *Boutiques selling gold jewellery are very popular among the Indians; a profusion of wares sold in Little India.*

offering cheap rates for overseas phone calls, which are frequented by the many Indian, Pakistani and Bangladeshi blue-collar workers that staff most of Singapore's construction companies. These single young men are there on any given Sunday, as they have made it a habit to visit this bustling area on their one day off each week.

Two must-see places in Little India are Sri Srinivasa Perumal Temple and Mustafa's. The former is one of Singapore's most important temples. Dedicated to Vishnu, it is the starting point of the annual Thaipusam festival that is held in January or February—a gory but fascinating ceremony during which devotees parade the streets with steel hooks and skewers piercing their faces and bodies. Sri Srinivasa Perumal was built in 1855, but back then, the temple consisted of only a simple prayer hall and a pond.

Thanks to construction throughout the 1990s, the temple is now ornate and elaborately decorated. Its gopuram—the tower at its main gate—rises 20 m (66 ft) high and consists of multiple tiers of sculpture.

In contrast, Mustafa's is another kind of temple—one that is dedicated to commerce. Mustafa's may just be Singapore's most famous homegrown store. What started as a small clothing store in 1971 grew to an area with 84 sq m (900 sq ft) in 1973, and now spreads across 13,935 sq m (150,000 sq ft) in two adjacent buildings and sells over 75,000 different items.

Open 24 hours a day, Mustafa's sells everything and anything, from fruit to electronics, cars, holiday packages, watches, clothes, electrical appliances, jewellery and pharmaceuticals. No other establishment comes close to being the kind of one-stop shop that this emporium is. Everything is on discount. But despite the low prices, Mustafa's is a highly profitable store with an annual turnover of approximately S$302 million. To ensure a steady flow of overseas business, Mustafa's runs a 130-room hotel in the same building as one of its two branches.

For great Indian cuisine, the best place to visit is Race Course Road parallel to Serangoon Road. Banana Leaf Apollo, Muthu's Curry—a popular place where fish head curry was reportedly invented—and Delhi, which specialises in Northern Indian fare, are some of the posh restaurants along this row.

arab street

The Malay quarter known as Arab Street, is also called Kampong Glam. This latter name is taken from its first residents, the Gelam tribe of sea gypsies. Raffles allotted this area to Sultan Hussein Mohammed Shah through a treaty, and decreed it as a Muslim settlement. This then attracted many Arab traders who began to settle here. The district's Middle Eastern roots are still evident through its streets' names: Baghdad Street, Muscat Street, Haji Lane and of course, Arab Street.

THIS PAGE (FROM LEFT): The Sri Veeramakaliamman Temple is the oldest Hindu temple in Little India; jade bangles sold at a shophouse store.

OPPOSITE (FROM LEFT): During the Thaipusam festival, devotees engage in ritual piercing to atone for their sins; a devotee rests after his vel skewers are removed.

In recent years, this area has been undergoing a quiet renaissance. New cafés, restaurants and shops slowly sprouting in the area have made the neighbourhood extremely popular among the young and hip. Haji Lane, in particular, has become a haven for creative types, what with its lifestyle stores including White Room, a sexy multibrand boutique, and Straits Records, one of the few music stores that specialises in independent bands. Samar, a café that is open 24 hours, is just a short walk away.

An interesting development worth a visit is the Malay Heritage Centre. It is located in the Istana Kampong Glam, which was once the home of the Sultan and, until recently, of his descendants. Built in 1843, this beautiful old mansion and its surrounding property have been restored and were reopened in 2005. The Malay Heritage Museum is located here.

This area is also the location where some of the best Muslim and Malay restaurants can be found. Kandahar Street, especially, has several fantastic places where foodies love to flock to. Zam Zam Restaurant on North Bridge Road is a humble café that some claim serves the best murtabak—a fried Indian bread stuffed with minced mutton or chicken, onions and eggs, and eaten with curry.

the best place to get fresh food

Chinatown, Little India and Arab Street each have at least one good wet market where most housewives and foodies go to buy fresh vegetables, seafood, and meat. Cheaper than supermarkets, they often offer a wider variety of local produce and products.

The markets in Chinatown Complex and Arab Street, as well as the Tekka Market in Little India are certainly worth a visit if one is interested to catch the sights, smells and sounds of an authentic, local wet market.

It's best to go early in the morning when the produce is the most fresh. These markets also have adjoining hawker centres that sell local street food, which in Singapore is clean, so there is no need to worry about getting a runny tummy.

a very busy social calendar

Singapore has an amazing number of festivals and celebrations that are as varied as the cultures that thrive in the small island-state. Some have fixed dates, while others such as Chinese New Year and Hari Raya, which follow non-Julian calendars, fluctuate annually.

Chinese New Year, celebrated in January or February, lasts for 14 days and marks the start of the new year for Chinese all over the world. During the first few days, family members visit each other, and unmarried relatives offer oranges to older, married couples and receive "ang pows"—red packets with money—in exchange. Chinatown is decked with colourful lights and decorations, and there are fireworks displays over the Singapore river every night during this festive period. The Chingay Parade, held on the 22nd day of the Chinese New Year, is the city's largest street parade. Originally a Chinese celebration, the Chingay Parade has become a multicultural extravaganza.

There is no fixed date for Hari Raya Haji, the celebration held for all Muslims who have made the pilgrimage to Mecca. Animals like sheep are ritually slaughtered and the meat distributed to the poor through various mosques. Other Muslims will spend the day praying or visiting relatives. Hari Raya Puasa, which also has no fixed date, marks the end of Ramadan, the month-long fasting period that Muslims go through every year.

The Great Singapore Sale happens from May to July, and it marks the two months when all shopping establishments go on sale. While not strictly a cultural event, the outrageous shopping discounts attract much buzz and excitement for both locals and tourists and have been known to unite people from different backgrounds—behind the cash register.

The Singapore Arts Festival held every June is a month-long performing cultural event that presents some of the world's best music, theatre and dance troupes. Asian and world premieres are often showcased in this event.

August is usually regarded as an unlucky month for the Chinese, because it is believed the gates of Hell open during this month and spirits—who are hungry after their impoverished time in Hell—are free to wander over the earth to seek food or revenge. The Hungry Ghost Festival is the closest equivalent to the western Halloween. It is during this time that Chinese remember their dead family members. By offering food to the deceased, they appease the spirits and ward off bad luck.

August 9 is National Day, an important event for Singaporeans. Billed as the biggest party of the year, it is celebrated with a huge performance staged by the Singapore Armed Forces that involves locals from all walks of life. There are cultural performances, musical skits by famous pop stars, military exercises including jet manoeuvres, and lots of fireworks, and the Prime Minister addresses the nation in a much-awaited speech.

The Moon Cake Festival, also known as Mid-Autumn Festival, is celebrated in September. During this time, the moon is at its fullest and brightest, making it an ideal time to celebrate the summer's harvest. This festival also commemorates the success of the uprising in China—patriot Zhu Yuan Zhang, whose secret plot to overthrow the tyrannical rule of the Yuan dynasty in the 14th century was passed to fellow rebels in moon cakes. Today, mooncakes with sweet red bean and lotus seed paste are exchanged as gifts.

Deepavali, celebrated in October or November, is also called the Festival of Lights, which celebrates the Hindu Lord Krishna's triumph over the demon Narakasura. During Deepavali, Indian families place oil lamps in front of their homes and visit other family members and friends.

The last big celebration of the year is Christmas, which comes in December. Although a Christian holiday, it has become an event the whole country celebrates regardless of religion. Orchard Road comes alive with lighs and decorations and shops across the city go on sale. It's a beautiful and memorable time to visit the Lion City.

THIS PAGE (CLOCKWISE FROM TOP): The Chinese burn paper models and props for the deceased during the Hungry Ghost Festival; Little India lights up for Deepavali, the Festival of Lights; lanterns for the Mid-Autumn Festival form a dreamy tableau.

OPPOSITE: A Chinese opera performance held during the Hungry Ghost Festival to provide entertainment to wandering ghosts.

...the whole country celebrates regardless of religion.

Hotel 1929

This boutique hotel is a sister establishment of New Majestic Hotel in Bukit Pasoh Road. Hotel 1929 occupies five shophouses just off the quaint Chinese enclave of Chinatown and gets its name from the year the buildings were constructed. It is a whimsical mix of Old World architecture and contemporary chic—a unique hotel that appeals to all types of travellers, including the seasoned ones.

Hotel 1929 is a five-minute cab ride away from the heart of the business district and a short walk from the buzzing clubs and restaurants along Club Street. It is close to where the action is, but is far enough to provide the peace and quiet its clients need at the end of the day.

The refurbished interiors mix classic designer furnishings with vintage pieces.

There are 32 rooms of which no two are alike. Each room has state-of-the-art facilities and amenities including flat-screen LCD TVs, digital phones, high-speed Internet access and clear glass bathrooms. Two of the suites have their own rooftop hot tubs. Set in tropical roof gardens, they overlook the bright lights of Chinatown and its environs.

Along the corridors are black and white pictures of Singapore as a young nation evolving in the early years of the 20th century. There are unusual classic chairs from the hotel owner's private collection, which include the Joseph Hoffman Kubus sofa designed in 1910, Arne Jacobsen Swan and Egg chairs and vintage Pierre Paulin Tulip chairs. Hotel 1929's art deco interiors and hotel concept

THIS PAGE (FROM TOP): The hotel's furnishings and fittings are an intriguing mix of modern and retro designs; bold shades and bright colours give this room a distinctive look.

OPPOSITE: The lobby is a showroom of the owner's collection of classic chairs.

...a whimsical mix of Old World architecture and contemporary chic...

have garnered favourable reviews from publications like *Harper's Bazaar*, *The Asian Wall Street Journal*, *The Washington Post*, *Condé Nast* and *Time Magazine*. The Urban Redevelopment Authority commended the hotel's solid foundation, use of roof space, the mirroring effect in its lobby, and the re-layout of the rooms, which created more rooms with views. Hotel 1929 was given the Architectural Heritage Award in 2003.

Hotel 1929 is also home to Ember. The avant-garde minimalist décor gives this 45-seat restaurant, lounge and bar an ambience usually found in a designer home. Well-heeled and trendy food and wine connoisseurs often flock to the restaurant, where modern European cuisine is given an Asian twist.

Two of the restaurant's must-try dishes are Oven-roasted Chilean Seabass with Ginger and Soy Broth and Lobster Gazpacho with Cucumber.

PHOTOGRAPHS COURTESY OF HOTEL 1929.

ROOMS	32 rooms • 3 suites
FOOD	Ember: modern European
DRINK	bar and lounge
FEATURES	selection of vintage chairs • rooftop jacuzzi • landscaped roof garden • laundry • mail service • car/limousine hire
BUSINESS	high-speed Internet access
NEARBY	Chinatown • Tanjong Pagar • Club Street • Ann Siang Hill
CONTACT	50 Keong Saik Road, Singapore 089154 • telephone: +65.6347 1929 • facsimile: +65.6327 1929 • email: reservations@hotel1929.com • website: www.hotel1929.com

The Scarlet

Singapore's latest boutique hotel, The Scarlet, is an 84-room establishment that mixes traditional shophouse architecture and contemporary design. It departs from the predictable mould of city hotels with its five themed suites whose names match the moods their interiors evoke.

Splendour, Passion, Opulent, Lavish and Swank each have different colour schemes, furnishings and amenities to match the themes. The Passion Suite, for example, was designed with honeymooners in mind. Its seductive burgundy, fuchsia, silver and black interiors have a low ceiling to create an intimate space. It has a canopied four-poster bed as well as an outdoor jacuzzi.

The 25 executive rooms and 14 premium rooms target business travellers. These rooms are equipped with facilities for guests who are working on the road. The

23 deluxe rooms and 13 standard rooms target tourists and travellers. People who spend the better part of the day sightseeing will appreciate the comfort offered by these accommodations. All rooms at The Scarlet, regardless of type, have individually controlled air-conditioning, cable TVs with complimentary movie channels, work desks with data ports for PC and fax connections, computerised wake-up call systems, voice mail message systems, personal bars, electronic door locks and digital in-room safes.

The Scarlet adds its special touch with its choice breakfast sets, a gourmet selection in the personal bar and evening cocktails, which are served in the rooms. It offers a choice between goose tempur and non-allergenic foam pillows, and has its own brand of bathroom amenities. Apart from DVD players, all rooms have free unlimited

THIS PAGE: *Opulence and elegance set The Scarlet apart from other boutique hotels; the careful selection of décor and furnishings provide a distinct ambience in the hotel's bar and in each of the suites.*

OPPOSITE: *The Scarlet is only a short walk away from the hip bars, clubs and restaurants frequented by nightowls.*

high-speed Internet access. The Sanctum, the hotel's oval-shaped boardroom, has luxurious furnishings and is equipped with modern conference facilities. The hotel shop, Flair, is the only gift store in Singapore which carries Spaceform stationery products from London. Furnishings in the suites and rooms may also be custom-ordered here. Other hotel amenities are likewise packaged as products with distinct identities. Flaunt is the hotel's gym, while Soda is the outdoor jacuzzi.

Desire is the hotel restaurant that offers Asian-inspired modern cuisine, Breeze is the Mediterranean-styled roof-top bar and grill and Bold is the hotel's bar. In the evenings, a pub crawl could start from Bold and move on to the many establishments along vibrant Club Street, a short walk from Erskine Road.

Situated in the city centre, The Scarlet is a good starting point for guests who want to go sightseeing. Chinatown, with its charming shophouses, is just a 10-minute walk; and the nearest MRT station is only 5 minutes on foot.

PHOTOGRAPHS COURTESY OF THE SCARLET.

FACTS		
ROOMS	84 rooms, including 5 suites	
FOOD	Desire: modern • Breeze: seafood and grills	
DRINK	premium wines and champagnes • cocktails	
FEATURES	individually-themed suites • rooftop jacuzzi • gym • laundry • mail • boutique gift shop	
BUSINESS	high-speed Internet access • business centre • conference room	
NEARBY	Chinatown • central business district • bars and clubs • dining	
CONTACT	33 Erskine Road, Singapore 069333 • telephone: +65.6511 3333 • facsimile: +65.6511 3303 • email: reservations@thescarlethotel.com, enquiry@thescarlethotel.com • website: www.thescarlethotel.com	

Bar SáVanh + IndoChine Club Street

Architectural Design Award in 2000 for this concept and design. It was also short-listed by the Singapore Tourism Board as 'Nightspot of the Year' in 2001.

The down-tempo tunes in Bar SáVanh's playlist are so popular that they have been included in the first CD compilation of the IndoChine Group, whose restaurants and bars are the preferred venue of discerning clientele. Bar SáVanh serves New and Old World wines from Australia, South Africa, Chile, New Zealand, California, France and Italy, as well as premium champagnes and sparkling wines. Vinto Terrino—its own concoction of red wine with fresh lime and soda—is extremely popular with young urban professionals.

Following drinks, patrons can head upstairs to the IndoChine Group's inaugural restaurant outlet, IndoChine

THIS PAGE (FROM TOP): The cosy space of Bar Sávanh; unusual features include greenery and a koi pond.

OPPOSITE (FROM LEFT): Dine in style at IndoChine Club Street, where Asian cuisine is given a western twist; a stylish space combining Buddhist art and western style furnishings.

Bar SáVanh in Club Street offers urbanites the perfect venue to unwind. Located near the central business district, this award-winning bar features a three-storey waterfall, sprawling koi pond, a 6-m (20-ft) long opium bed and replicas of some of Indochina's finest ancient artefacts. The sweet scent of jasmine incense add to the tranquil ambience of this lush sanctuary. Bar SáVanh clinched the prestigious

Club Street. Chefs use the freshest herbs and spices from the Mekong Delta trinity of Cambodia, Laos and Vietnam to recreate the street food of Phnom Penh, Vientiane and Luang Phrabang. Food and art harmonise as the fare, which was introduced to Singapore by IndoChine Club Street, is served in a setting decorated with bold Asian sculptures and furnishings. The aromatic garlic butter prawns of Danang and the sesame lamb tenderloin scented with lemongrass come highly recommended by food critics. Vegetarians will also be able to sample a variety of dishes such as the unique pomelo salad of Saigon and steamed mushrooms Sam Neua-style.

The Club by Aphrodisiac gave Singapore its first martini and champagne bar. Blue light glows from tabletops and marine life serves as a magnificent backdrop for the dance floor. The food, cocktails and shots are aphrodisiacs all, from the shot of Killer Instinct containing snake wine with ginseng and exotic herbs.

CoChine Gallery on the third floor makes a stylish venue for private functions and corporate events. It stages exhibits of Asian art, which are available for purchase.

FACTS		
SEATS	Bar SáVanh: 80 • IndoChine Club Street: 120 • The Club: 70 • CoChine Gallery: 50
FOOD	contemporary Indochinese
DRINK	Old and New World wines • cocktails • beer
FEATURES	interior waterfall • koi pond • ancient artefacts
NEARBY	Raffles Place • Far East Square • China Square • Chinatown
CONTACT	47–49 Club Street, East Chinatown, Singapore 069424 • telephone: +65.6323 0145 (Bar SáVanh), +65.6323 0503 (IndoChine Restaurant), +65.6325 8529 (The Club by Aphrodisiac), +65.6323 1043 (CoChine Gallery) • facsimile: +65.6323 2417 • email: enquiry@indochine.com.sg • website: www.indochine.com.sg/clubst.htm

PHOTOGRAPHS COURTESY OF INDOCHINE GROUP AND MING.

Oso Ristorante

THIS PAGE (FROM TOP): *The warm yellow lighting complements the splashes of red and brown hues in the dining area; the cheese menu includes gorgonzola, Taleggio, truffle-infused cheese and other imported Italian cheeses.*

OPPOSITE: *The casual atmosphere in the bar area encourages interaction among guests.*

Oso Ristorante, a finalist in the World Gourmet Summit for Best Chef, Best Manager and Best New Restaurant, is a partnership between wine connoisseur Stephane Colleoni and Chef Diego Chiarini. 'Oso', which means 'try' in Italian, is an invitation to sample the authentic Italian dining experience in the duo's restaurant in Tanjong Pagar.

At the entrance is a modern bar with comfortable sofas, where patrons can wait to be seated or linger for after-dinner drinks. The 60-seat dining area has contemporary décor and mood lighting. Its intimate ambience complements the delectable modern Italian cuisine served here. A wide variety of cured meat and cheese is stored in a climate-controlled room—a first in Singapore.

The wine cellar, which also doubles as a private dining room for six, has over 250 bottles of champagne and rare and vintage

red wines—a collection that Oso is famous for. On the menu are homemade creations like the cured beef antipasti and different types of pasta. Careful cooking is evident in the Lamb Rack with Black Onions and Salsifis, which is baked for 8 hours. Rigatoni with Braised Rabbit, Thyme and Black Olives and the Linguine with Fresh Baby Clams, Garlic and Basil Pesto Sauce are two favourites among diners. Gelato, sherbet and desserts end a meal on a high note. Apart from all-time favourite flavours, the gelato and sherbet come in interesting new tastes: cinnamon, pink grapefruit and mint. The selection of desserts includes Hot Dark Chocolate Tart Crostata served warm with pistachio ice cream, Sicilian Cannoli filled with Ricotta Cheese and Mixed Candied Fruit, and Panna Cotta with Black Pepper Caramel Sauce and Fruit.

Chiarini's years of experience come from working in Four Seasons Hotel in Tokyo and Hotel de Paris in Monaco with Alain Ducasse. Colleoni's experience in restaurant service was honed in restaurants such as Martinez Hotel in Cannes, and Savoy Hotel in London. He also worked at Bice Restaurant and Le Jules Vernes Restaurant in the Eiffel Tower, both in Paris. Together, their work earned Oso several 'Awards of Excellence' from the World Gourmet Summit and recognition from *Wine & Dine* as 'Singapore's Top Restaurant'. The culinary expertise and excellent service for which Oso is known also extends outside the restaurant and to the events where it provides catering services. Oso Ristorante is open for lunch from 12.30 pm to 2.30 pm from Mondays to Fridays and for dinner from 6.30 pm to 10.30 pm everyday including public holidays. Oso Privato, a function room located opposite the restaurant, accommodates 18 to 40 guests. Reservations are encouraged.

FACTS

SEATS	restaurant: 60 • private dining room: 6 • Oso Privato: 18–40
FOOD	contemporary Italian
DRINK	modern Italian bar
FEATURES	cheese room • set menus • catering
NEARBY	Club Street • Chinatown • bars • restaurants • sightseeing • city tours
CONTACT	Oso Ristorante, 27 Tanjong Pagar Road, Singapore 088450 • Oso Privato, 66 Tanjong Pagar Road, Singapore 088450 • telephone: +65.6327 8378 • facsimile: +65.6327 8498 • email: oso27@singnet.com.sg • website: www.oso.sg

PHOTOGRAPHS COURTESY OF DIEGO CHIARINI AND STEPHANE COLLEONI.

Senso Ristorante + Bar

Senso Ristorante + Bar is a six-year old establishment in Club Street which provides world-class Italian dining.

Their Master Chef is an Italian native whose cooking experience comes from many kitchens all over Europe. Working in collaboration with him is the resident sommelier, who chooses the best wine to complement the dishes.

There are over 250 wine labels in Senso's walk-in temperature-controlled cellar. Senso has the largest selection of Super Tuscan wines, which include Tignanello, Solaia, Ornellaia and Sassicaia. The extensive wine list consists of Old and New World labels, vintages from Gaja and Antinori and perhaps the oldest Barolo in Southeast Asia—the 1924 Barolo Borgogno Reserved.

Among the innovative dishes Senso offers is its popular Carnaroli Risotto with Italian Champagne and Sautéed Prawns. The Tiramisu, one of the chef's selections, is made from his own family recipe. Set menus are available for groups of a minumum of 12 persons. These menus are updated

THIS PAGE: The dining area glows with warm yellow light.

OPPOSITE (FROM LEFT): Contemporary design was used in the interiors of this former convent; a bright and pleasant area for communal dining.

Senso...embodies la dolce vita...

friends are meant to be cherished in the same way the food and wine are meant to be comsumed: at an unhurried pace.

Reservations are encouraged at Senso, which is open for lunch and dinner from Monday to Friday, and dinner only on Saturdays, Sundays and public holidays. It also has an outlet in Geneva.

regularly: the set lunch menu is changed every week while the set dinner menu is changed every month—all the more reason to make frequent visits.

There is one beautiful private room that accommodates up to 25 persons—very popular for intimate events and business meetings. Diners can enjoy a signature grappa at the luminous bar, or lounge in the leather sofas near it. Outside is a patio where a reproduction of

a Michelangelo sculpture stands. Laid-back and elegant at the same time, the architecture of this space resembles a Tuscan courtyard.

Every year since it opened, Senso has earned several awards and recognition for its restaurant design, cuisine and service from the World Gourmet Summit, *Wine & Dine Magazine*, *Singapore Tatler*, *Wine & Dine Guide* and *The Wine Review*.

Senso, which is Italian for 'senses', embodies la dolce vita—the company of

FACTS		
	SEATS	restaurant: 120 • courtyard: 40 • bar: 40 • combined standing room for 400
	FOOD	contemporary Italian
	DRINK	extensive wine list • bar
	FEATURES	private room • courtyard
	NEARBY	Chinatown • Tanjong Pagar • Ann Siang Hill • Central Business District
	CONTACT	21 Club Street, Singapore 069410 • telephone: +65.6224 3534 • facsimile: +65.6224 5508 • email: senso@singnet.com.sg • website: www.senso.sg

PHOTOGRAPHS COURTESY OF SENSO RISTORANTE + BAR.

Beaujolais Wine Bar

A quaint Chinese shophouse in Ann Siang Hill has been tastefully restored and converted into what is now Beaujolais Wine Bar. The selection of wines from around the world, candlelit ambience and bistro food make this French wine bar an ideal place to unwind after work, relax after a day of sightseeing, or meet for a romantic tête-à-tête.

Unlike most wine bars, Beaujolais does not intimidate with long wine lists. Customers can peruse its list of wines, or simply walk to the shelves and choose from the extensive and well-sourced collection.

Connoisseurs will be glad to know that Beaujolais offers French cheeses, pâté, garlic mushrooms and tomato bruschetta to complement their wines. A tip from regulars is to check with the friendly staff for the wine of the month, which is offered at discounted prices.

French cuisine and Italian hors d'oeuvres can be enjoyed indoors, where diners can admire the display of artwork

THIS PAGE: A slice of Europe in a quaint Chinatown shophouse.

OPPOSITE (FROM LEFT): Beaujolais' charming façade conjures summer's lazy afternoons.

and listen to jazz and the blues. As is typical of food establishments in Paris, Beaujolais also has ample al fresco seating.

Bankers and advertising executives in the area make up most of Beaujolais' group of regulars. People whose offices are in nearby Club Street hop over for espresso or for pre-dinner drinks with their clients. European expatriates who miss home take in the charming atmosphere that is reminiscent of a café in their side of the world. The old fashioned romantic ambience makes it popular among couples. Since it is just a five-minute stroll from Chinatown and a short distance from the Scarlet Hotel, Beaujolais also attracts a fair amount of tourists.

Beaujolais has been around for 11 years and is counted as one of the authentic wine bars sprouting in the area. It is available for private gatherings and functions, providing service that is both professional and affordable.

FACTS

SEATS	50
FOOD	French and Italian
DRINK	Old and New World wines • cocktails • beer
FEATURES	wine cellar
NEARBY	Maxwell Market • Club Street • Chinatown
CONTACT	1 Ann Siang Hill, Singapore 069784 • telephone: +65.6224 2227 • facsimile: +65.6324 4787 • email: beaujolais@mac.com

PHOTOGRAPHS COURTESY OF BEAUJOLAIS WINE BAR.

W Wine Bar

W Wine Bar along Club Street is another interesting addition to the stretch of historical shophouses that have been transformed into trendy lifestyle shops, fine dining restaurants and bars.

It occupies the ground level of a shophouse, with a glass façade that blurs the boundary between its interior and exterior spaces. The glass doors can be slid back completely to let in the air and the vibe of energetic Club Street—guests find that this also gives a good view for people-watching.

Ambient lights illuminate the interiors, which are a blend of pale stone, clear glass and dark wood. Maroon and pebble-coloured velvet couches are arranged to create comfortable spaces for quiet business meetings. The plush seating and convivial atmosphere also make it an ideal venue for informal drinks and get-togethers—lounge music is set at a volume that does not overpower conversations.

There are over 200 vintage and non-vintage wines in W Wine Bar's temperature-controlled walk-in cellar. Guests are welcome to take a closer look at the labels available. There are Australian wines like Cloudy Bay, Cape Mentelle and Yalumba; French wines like Chateau Cheval Blanc, Louis Latour and Dujac; and sweet wines like Chateau D'Yquem. Moet & Chandon and Krug lead its list of

THIS PAGE: *A cosy atmosphere that encourages conversation.*

OPPOSITE: *Wine lovers flock here to share and learn about the finer aspects of drinking wine.*

...over 200 vintage and non-vintage wines...cocktails, cognac, sherry, reserve whiskeys...

beverage establishments could complement each other more perfectly. Guests at W Wine Bar who plan to move to Senso for dinner can arrange to have their drinks brought over.

W Wine Bar is available for corporate functions, intimate wine-tasting events and parties. It also offers customised packages.

champagnes. The bar also has other beverages apart from wine. There is a large selection of cocktails, cognac, sherry, reserve whiskeys and Scotland's best single malt whisky, The Macallan. Those who want to have light snacks to go with their drinks can choose from the menu of finger food. Cigar lovers, on the other hand, will find a range of Havana cigars such as Cohiba, Montecristo and Partagas at the bar.

Every month, W Wine Bar organises regular wine-tasting events for its regulars and other wine aficionados. During these wine appreciation sessions, the on-site sommelier shares the depth of his knowledge with the guests. With the well-stocked cellar to back him up, it is not very difficult to impress his audience.

W Wine Bar is affiliated with Senso Ristorante next door. No two food and

FACTS		
	SEATS	30
	FOOD	finger food
	DRINK	over 200 vintage and non-vintage labels • full-service bar
	FEATURES	walk-in wine cellar
	NEARBY	Chinatown • Tanjong Pagar • Ann Siang Hill
	CONTACT	11 Club Street, Singapore 069405 • telephone: +65.6223 3886 • facsimile: +65.6223 5233 • email: gina@senso.com.sg • website: www.wwinebar.sg

PHOTOGRAPHS COURTESY OF W WINE BAR.

Vanilla Home

Fashionistas, interior designers and architects have beaten a path to this restored double-storey shophouse in Club Street for its impeccable merchandise. Offering exquisite interior products, Vanilla Home specialises in decorative lighting, furniture and accessories from Europe's top design houses. The look is essentially contemporary classic—elegant and luxurious without being glitzy. The creative force behind Vanilla Home is Stefanie Hauger and Rebecca Metcalfe who have established a reputation for importing exclusively from leading European brand names. It is their hand-picked selection that strikes a chord with discerning fans. The showroom is a veritable jewel box of visual seductiveness, constantly evolving as new designs are showcased in the region for the first time.

Vanilla Home is deliberately designed not to look like a shop. Instead, it is a unique shopping environment where clients are encouraged to browse. Timeless and chic, informal yet structured, it is a welcoming space with an emphasis on decorative lighting. Guaranteed showstoppers from the UK include lamps with breathtaking sculptural silhouettes from Porta Romana and new mirrored and printed glass furniture by Knowles & Christou. Not to be missed are the Venetian silk pendants originally designed by Italian maestro Mariano Fortuny and meticulously recreated by Venetia Studium.

...a touch of understated opulence...

Eye-catching lead crystal lamps by British designer Emily Todhunter bring a touch of understated opulence, while a collaboration with renowned glass-blower Anthony Stern has produced translucent pieces of exceptional beauty.

For sleek lines and finishes, look no further than fabulous furniture and decorative lighting from William Yeoward and Nicholas Haslam. For a more relaxed style, Original BTC lamps incorporate materials such as bone china and enamel.

Vanilla Home has everything you need for a truly glamorous lifestyle. For cosmopolitan crystalware, there is David Redman's latest range in amethyst and black which includes martini glasses, champagne flutes and a cocktail shaker. For the table, Limoges porcelain in an array of mouth-watering tones by Harlequin Tabletop match virtually any colour scheme. Couples who are setting up a home together can also register a Vanilla Home Wedding List. The Vanilla Home brand is expanding its own design repertoire as well. Recent additions include Talitha cushions scattered with semi-precious stones and upholstered furniture that emphasises comfort. It also supports talent across a wide spectrum from jewellery by Lesli Berggren to stunning art from Irene Hauger and Ketna Patel.

Today, Vanilla Home has gained respect for sourcing products of exceptional quality. They now grace some of the most beautiful interiors in the region including hotels, resorts, showflats and private residences.

THIS PAGE: *These lamps are meant to be regarded not just as fixtures but also as works of art.*

OPPOSITE: *Pieces of superlative craftsmanship that exude timeless style make good investments.*

FACTS

PRODUCTS	decorative lamps • furniture • soft furnishings • porcelain • crystalware • artwork • jewellery
FEATURES	imported European designs • wedding list
NEARBY	Chinatown • Tanjong Pagar • Ann Siang Hill • central business district
CONTACT	48 Club Street, Singapore 069425 • telephone: +65.6324 6206 • facsimile: +65.6324 6207 • email: contact@vanilla-home.com • website: www.vanilla-home.com

PHOTOGRAPHS COURTESY OF VANILLA HOME.

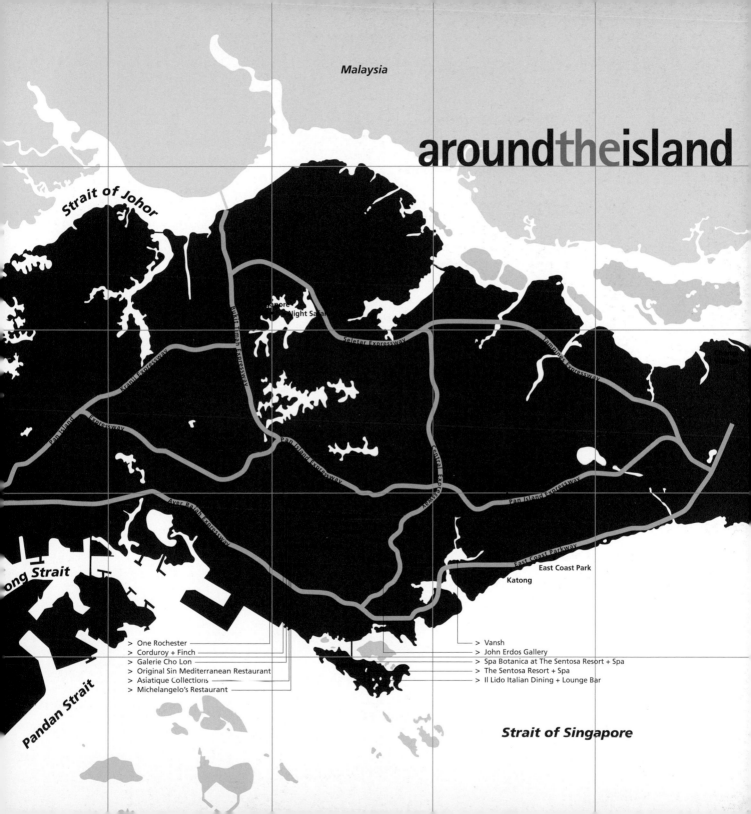

aroundtheisland

Malaysia

Strait of Johor

ong Strait

Pandan Strait

Singapore
Night Safari

Bukit Timah Expressway

Kranji Expressway

Pan Island Expressway

Pan Island Expressway

Ayer Rajah Expressway

Seletar Expressway

Tampines Expressway

Central Expressway

Pan Island Expressway

East Coast Parkway

East Coast Park

Katong

> One Rochester
> Corduroy + Finch
> Galerie Cho Lon
> Original Sin Mediterranean Restaurant
> Asiatique Collections
> Michelangelo's Restaurant

> Vansh
> John Erdos Gallery
> Spa Botanica at The Sentosa Resort + Spa
> The Sentosa Resort + Spa
> Il Lido Italian Dining + Lounge Bar

Strait of Singapore

around the island

Not all of Singapore's attractions and places of interest are in the city centre. Visitors who go beyond token visits to must-see locations will have more than just generic souvenirs to take home. Those who take the time to explore some of the outlying areas are often rewarded by what they discover.

sentosa

Just 500 m (1,640 ft) off the southern coast of Singapore is the tiny island of Sentosa. Originally called Pulau Blakang Mati ("The Island of Death Behind"), it measures only 3 km (2 miles) by 1 km (0.6 mile). Despite its size, Sentosa is one of Singapore's most popular spots for both locals and tourists. Up to World War II, the British used the island as a military base. Today, the island has been transformed into a recreational playground with a variety of attractions. Fort Siloso, Underwater World and the "Images of Singapore" exhibition are among the interesting places worth a visit for families.

Fort Siloso was Britain's main naval defence point from the 1880s until World War II. The Fort's gun emplacements guarded Singapore's waters and discouraged attacks from the west. However, when the Japanese invaded Singapore, they came not from the sea but from land—on bicycles. Children and adults alike will be awed by the myriad sea creatures at Underwater World. Watch kids (and maybe some adults too) squeal with delight as they get to feel starfish, stingrays and even baby sharks at the touch pool—a wet and fun way to start a visit to this popular oceanarium. With 2,500 marine life from 250 different species, they can be observed from within an 83-m (272-ft) acrylic tunnel.

"Images of Singapore" has three main exhibits that stage Singapore's past as a British trading port, its war years from 1941 to 1945 and its multicultural festivals. Wax and animatronic figures, dioramas, replicas of artefacts and reproductions of locations breathe life into this remarkable presentation of the country's history.

PAGE 190: *A leisurely cable car ride in the sunset.*

THIS PAGE: *Located just a short distance off the southern coast of Singapore, Sentosa is a highly accessible and popular tourist destination.*

OPPOSITE: *Dancing lights of Sentosa's musical fountain.*

Young adults have made the island's beaches—notably Siloso, Tanjong and Palawan—their weekend home. Bikini-clad bodies and their male counterparts have been flocking to a number of new, cool beach bars, clubs and restaurants. They'll eat, drink, dance, play volleyball, show off their bodies and work on their tans. The most popular of them all is KM8 located on Tanjong beach.

Sentosa has two 18-hole golf courses, as well as several hotels and spas. Recent developments are changing the island radically. S$8 billion are being poured into remaking Sentosa, creating a new luxury residential and retail zone called Sentosa Cove, a brand new cruise centre, a luxury marina, and a new and improved Harbourfront precinct.

The Harbourfront precinct will comprise offices, cruise and ferry terminals; Singapore's only cableway system, a multi-concept entertainment hub in a heritage building, and VivoCity, Singapore's largest retail and lifestyle mall. It is hoped that this development will attract more than 30 million visitors annually, including passengers at the Singapore Cruise Centre.

singapore zoo

Singapore has one of the world's best zoos. Animals roam in open-air enclosures with natural barriers of rock and vegetation. The zoo has over 2,000 animals of over 240 species, 40 of which are endangered species.

In addition to viewing the enclosures, visitors can also watch several entertaining shows and even interact with some of the animals. One of the zoo's most popular programmes is breakfast with the orang utans. With much to see and do, we recommend allocating half a day for a visit to the zoo.

night safari

Opposite the zoo is one of the truly unique attractions in Singapore— the Night Safari is the world's first wildlife park built for visitors at night. As approximately 90 per cent of the world's animals are nocturnal, the Night Safari is an innovative way to watch the animals when they are most active.

The park has over 1,200 animals of over 110 species, with strategic and specially-designed lighting and enclosures that allow visitors to view the animals closer than they would ever be able to in the wild. The leopard feeding is a popular attraction that can be witnessed from behind a large one-way mirror. Visitors can choose to explore the area on foot, or take a tram ride around the park.

jurong bird park

There are over 8,000 birds of more than 600 species living in this large theme park in Jurong. Many of these beautiful and exotic birds are endangered. The park itself is worth visiting to take in its gorgeous landscape design. Kids will enjoy the many shows that take place throughout the day, especially the Birds of Prey show where trained eagles, falcons and hawks show off their predatory skills.

The Botanic Gardens is only a 15-minute walk or a few minutes' drive from Orchard Road.

singapore botanic gardens

One of the most beautiful and serene parts of Singapore, the Botanic Gardens off Holland Road is only a 15-minute walk or a few minutes' drive from bustling Orchard Road. Covering 53 hectares (130 acres), the park is divided into various areas. The National Orchid Garden, one of only two areas in the park that charge admission, is definitely worth a visit.

On weekends, visitors often stumble upon a free outdoor concert. The Symphony Stage hosts such performances by various groups, from the Singapore Symphony Orchestra to foreign jazz and salsa bands. Early in the morning, between 6 am and 8 am, one may chance upon the who's who of Singapore's elite at the park; many of the city's top citizens to take a walk in the gardens before starting their day.

bukit timah nature reserve

Nature buffs who love to hike can just put on their hiking boots and get to the Bukit Timah Nature Reserve in minutes. This 164-hectare (405-acre) park is only 12 km (7 miles) away from the city centre. Most visitors and even many locals have no idea that there are still parts of Singapore covered in rain forest, this park being one of them. Apart from offering several excellent nature walks and jungle trails, the reserve has also opened a tower and treetop walk that gives stunning views of the park and the rest of the island.

fort canning park

This small park was built on a hill in one of Singapore's most historic sites. This area was believed to be the site of the palace of Parameswara, a Palembang ruler in the 14th century. Later, the hill area known as Bukit Larangan (Forbidden Hill) became

THIS PAGE (FROM TOP): The soothing and quiet charm of the Botanic Gardens; get close to nature at the Bukit Timah Nature Reserve.

OPPOSITE: Elegant trees and orchids at the Botanic Gardens.

the site of the island's first Christian cemetery. When Raffles came to Singapore, he built his residence here in 1822. The house later became the Government House, which was eventually replaced with a British fort—Fort Canning—that stood here from 1861 to 1926.

Today, little remains of either the palace or the British regime. There is a small plot known as the Keramat, or holy place. This is believed to be the burial place of the last king of the Temasek kingdom.

The two Gothic gates at the park entrances, believed to have been designed by government engineer Captain Charles Faber, were built in 1846. The only remnant of the British Fort is part of the old Fort Gate and Fort Wall at the

top of the hill. In 1926, the British built a huge army barracks on top of the hill. Today, the Fort Canning Centre houses the Singapore Dance Theatre and a cooking school called at-sunrise. Across from the centre is the Battle Box, a guided tour of the British underground command centre. The tour recounts the events of February 15, 1942, the day the British surrendered to the Japanese.

east coast park

This 10-km (6-mile) stretch of beach along Singapore's eastern shore has been transformed into a family-oriented recreational zone, complete with barbecue pits, a sailing and windsurfing centre, walking trails and bike/rollerblade trails, a very popular seafood centre, a water-based theme park, a tennis centre, several other cafés and restaurants, and holiday chalets. East Coast Park is always bustling with activity: families camp here, teenagers congregate in droves, dog owners bring

THIS PAGE (FROM TOP): The Fort Canning Centre is home to the Singapore Dance Theatre; the old Fort Gate is a remnant of the British Fort built in the 18th century.

OPPOSITE (FROM TOP): Beach goers enjoying the cool sea breeze and beautiful sunset at East Coast Park; a child busies himself with building sandcastles.

their pets to play in the surf, and others come for the sun and good food. Visitors interested in trying Chilli Crab or Pepper Crab, both popular local dishes, should make their way to the East Coast Seafood Centre.

This complex houses several good seafood restaurants that offer everything from crab dishes to barbecued stingray and many other local delights. Some of these establishments however, like to take advantage of naïve travellers, so it's a good idea to ask for a menu with prices or confirm the amount on the bill upon ordering.

holland village

One of the most popular and relaxing neighborhoods in Singapore is a small pocket of suburban cool off Holland Road. Holland Village is a self-contained bohemian haven filled with restaurants, pubs, shops and homes. The Holland Village Shopping Centre has many arts and crafts stores and was once the heart of

THIS PAGE (FROM TOP): Al fresco restaurants and pubs line the streets at Holland Village; looking at the crowd it packs nightly, "Chomp Chomp" is still one of Singapore's most well-loved hawker centres.

OPPOSITE (CLOCKWISE FROM LEFT): Indulge in delicious local Malay food such as satay at Geylang; many Peranakan families have set up homes in shophouses in Katong for generations; Rumah Bebe in Katong sells traditional Peranakan art, textiles, jewellery and more.

the area. These days, the shops that line the nearby side streets of Lorong Liput and Lorong Mambong are getting more attention. Some restaurants, pubs and cafés there stay open till the early hours of the morning, to cater to late-night party goers and night owls who can be found chatting and chilling out with a hot cuppa or a cold beer.

Wala Wala Café Bar, one of the most established pubs at Holland Village, is clearly a firm favourite among residents and visitors. It is packed almost every night, and especially on evenings when there are live gigs performed by local bands. The hip and fashion-conscious can be seen flocking to boutique shops that carry designs and labels by edgy, independent Australian designers, and furniture shops selling hard-to-find items such as those by cult Hong Kong design house G.O.D.

Across Holland Avenue, what was once a purely residential area—sleepy Chip Bee Gardens—has become home to several chic restaurants, shops, galleries and other lifestyle purveyors, such as antique shops and cooking schools. One of the popular establishments here is Shermay's Cooking School. Its owner, Shermay Lee, is the author of the revised Mrs Lee Cookbooks—originally written by her grandmother—that are considered as some of the most authoritative texts on Peranakan and local cuisine. In addition to Ms Lee, several of the country's best chefs teach at this small but impressive cooking school.

serangoon gardens

Serangoon Gardens is one of Singapore's most popular residential suburbs. Two of the country's best hawker centres are located here: the Serangoon Gardens Food Centre, nicknamed "Chomp Chomp" by locals, and the

Serangoon Gardens Market's food court. Locals flock to these stalls when seeking authentic and delicious variations on some classic hawker dishes.

katong

To experience a bit more of the Peranakan culture, head to this neighbourhood in the eastern part of Singapore. Many Peranakan or Straits Chinese-families have made their homes in this part of the island for generations. The side streets that intersect Joo Chiat and East Coast Roads showcase stunning examples of the kinds of shophouses that the Peranakans built and have lived in.

Joo Chiat is a food mecca for foodies. Some of the best examples of Nonya cuisine—the Peranakan style of

cooking—can be found in the number of restaurants that pepper this long road. Some, like the amazing Guan Ho Soon, have been there since the 1950s.

Over the past few years, though, Joo Chiat Road has become a little less innocent than it once was. A number of budget hotels, bars and karaoke lounges have opened, catalysing a new nightlife in this once-quiet area.

geylang

Like Katong, Geylang is one of the older residential suburbs in Singapore. While a large Peranakan community made Katong their home, Malays settled in Geylang.

Geylang Serai, the central market, is where the Malay influences are most apparent; many of the shops and food stalls here cater to Malay tastes. A "Malay Cultural Village" is also nearby, a cultural centre that opened in 1990.

Foodies claim that the local fare and street food in this neighbourhood as the best in Singapore. In fact, famous chef and TV personality Anthony Bourdain went so far as to say that the best restaurant in Singapore is a small, open-air coffee shop called Sin Huat Eating House, at the corner of Geylang Road and Geylang Lorong 35. While modest in appearance, Sin Huat Eating House serves some of the freshest seafood in the country. Chef Danny Yong's signature dish of Sri Lankan crabs fried with rice vermicelli has made him a legend in Singapore and has been mentioned in international publications such as the *New York Times* and *Gourmet Magazine*. Many of the cafés and roadside restaurants stay open till late, while

others welcome patrons until the wee hours of the morning. Such late operating hours are tied to the second reason why this neighbourhood is not just famous, but bustling, every night. Geylang is the location to find some of Singapore's most happening bars, pubs and karaoke lounges.

changi village

This idyllic and peaceful neighbourhood gives visitors a rare glimpse of what Singapore must have been like 20 years ago. Located in the east, near the airport and the beach, this quiet enclave is the ideal location for a long, al fresco lunch. Much like a laidback

TOP: *In the day, the quiet façade of Geylang belies its colourful and lively nature at night.*
OPPOSITE: *Durians are widely sold in Geylang.*

THIS PAGE (FROM TOP): *A gem of a starfish found on the shore at Changi Beach; narrow planks now mark the place where visitors used to take bumboats to Pulau Ubin.*
OPPOSITE: *The open-air Changi Chapel exudes a sense of calm and peace.*

village most people visit during weekends and public holidays for some peace and sea breeze, Changi Village is the perfect place to go to if you want to kick back and unwind. Feast on local favourite delights such as nasi lemak at the hawker centre or fish and chips at the famous Charlie's Corner, relax and spend time with family and loved ones in holiday chalets, or go fishing by the sea at the tranquil Changi Beach Park.

For nature lovers, taking a stroll along the Changi Boardwalk, which stretches from the Changi Beach Club to Changi Sailing Club, is a treat for the eyes. Made up of four segments, the boardwalk takes visitors on a scenic journey: Sunset Walk has a splendid view of the sea at Changi Point; Kelong Walk has its boardwalk with kelong stilts built over water that brings one back to those good old fishing village days; Cliff Walk lets one enjoy a walk through lush greenery; and Sailing Point Walk provide panoramic sea views near the Changi Sailing Club.

At The Changi Museum, visitors take another kind of walk, down memory lane. The Museum documents significant events that happened during the Japanese Occupation, and thus serves as an important education and resource centre. Old-timers will be interested in the fact that Changi Prison was used as a prisoner-of-war (POW) camp during World War II. As many as 3,000 civilian prisoners were held in this penitentiary, which was meant to accommodate no more than 600 at a time. Younger travellers will be amused to know that Changi Prison was where "rogue banker" Nick Leeson—the man who brought down Baring's bank—was jailed. The Changi Chapel, which symbolised the many chapels that Changi POWs had built, is an important monument dedicated to those who maintained their faith and dignity in the face of adversity during those dark years of the Japanese Occupation.

The new Changi Point Ferry Terminal replaces the former old jetty shed at Sungei Changi as the gateway to Pulau Ubin, a rustic, off-the-beaten-track island rich in ecological diversity, a mere 10-minute ride away. An increased interest in Chek Jawa, a newly-discovered eco-haven at Pulau Ubin, led to the building of the new ferry terminal to meet the rise in the number of visitors.

The Changi Chapel is an important monument to believers during the Japanese Occupation.

The Sentosa Resort + Spa

The Sentosa Resort & Spa is a luxury five-star resort that is an outstanding example of tropical architecture. It is one of Asia's best kept secrets, with Singapore's first garden destination spa, Spa Botanica.

The thoughtful integration of nature with living space resonates throughout this 11-hectare (27-acre) sanctuary: it is surrounded by decades-old native trees, with koi ponds along the corridors leading to the deluxe rooms and suites. The open concept design ensures cool breezes throughout, creating a distinct sense of oneness with nature.

The low-rise colonial style resort has 167 deluxe rooms and 43 suites with views of luscious greenery. The designer rooms' elegant fittings and teak furniture blend with the plush interiors' refreshing hues. The celadon-tiled bathrooms have full-sized bathtubs and separate shower areas. The spacious living rooms of the suites are perfect for intimate gatherings or small meetings. All rooms and suites feature high-speed Internet access and state-of-the-art entertainment systems that include 42-inch plasma TVs—a first amongst luxury hotels in Singapore. Four garden villas located in a

secluded section of the resort offer total privacy. Each has its own driveway, living room and two bedrooms that open to a terrace with a midnight blue swimming pool and immaculately manicured foliage.

Dining options range from smart casual to elegant. The Terrace serves sumptuous international buffets, while fine dining restaurant The Cliff offers contemporary cuisine inspired by the sea. At The Pavilion, an open-air lounge, guests can sit back with cocktails while watching the sunset.

The serenity of the resort and the attentiveness of the staff add to its charm. Couples can look forward to spending time together in this romantic haven. Golf enthusiasts will find two 18-hole championship courses at the Sentosa Golf Club next door. Families will find it within close proximity to beaches and Sentosa's other interesting attractions. Day-trippers can take a breather

...thoughtful integration of nature with living space...

THIS PAGE (FROM TOP): The Cliff, an al fresco restaurant overlooking the South China sea, serves modern cuisine; the Grand Salon, one of the resort's meeting rooms, has a fantastic view of the sea.

OPPOSITE (FROM TOP): The open plan style of the Junior Suite; the bedroom of this Deluxe Suite gets a good share of breeze and natural light.

in Singapore's only tropical garden spa within the grounds. Corporate clients will find the elegant double-storey conference centre an ideal venue for conventions, conferences and corporate retreats. It has excellent facilities and over 1,300 sq m (13,993 sq ft) of flexible meeting space for groups of 20 to 400. Function rooms have natural lighting and great sea views, providing a creative environment where a balance of living, learning and leisure is achieved. Team building programmes can also be arranged within the island resort.

Winner of 'Singapore's Leading Spa Resort' by World Travel Awards, The Sentosa Resort & Spa was the first hotel in Singapore to be a distinguished member of the Small Luxury Hotels of the World, which represents the most luxurious and unique independent hotels and resorts.

FACTS		
ROOMS	167 deluxe rooms • 43 suites • 4 garden villas	
FOOD	The Terrace: international lunch buffet, barbecue dinner buffet, western and Asian à la carte • The Cliff: contemporary cuisine inspired by the sea	
DRINK	The Pavilion	
FEATURES	tennis courts • midnight blue swimming pool • gym and fitness centre • wedding and banquet planning and facilities • biking and jogging routes • conference centre • high-speed Internet access • teambuilding programmes	
NEARBY	Spa Botanica • Seven Eden Wellness Centre • Sentosa Golf Club • Tanjong Beach	
CONTACT	2 Bukit Manis Road, Sentosa Island, Singapore 099891 • telephone: +65.6275 0331 • facsimile: +65.6275 0228 • email: info@thesentosa.com • website: www.thesentosa.com	

PHOTOGRAPHS COURTESY OF THE SENTOSA RESORT + SPA.

Spa Botanica at The Sentosa Resort + Spa

Set in the grounds of The Sentosa Resort & Spa is Spa Botanica, Singapore's first and only garden destination spa. This luxurious wellness centre was once a 19th-century British army barrack that was transformed to house 15 indoor treatment rooms and suites as well as 6 outdoor pavilions. Meticulous restoration was done on the colonial architecture and façade, including the rows of crossed balustrades—a distinctive feature of British military barracks from that era. It earned The Sentosa Resort & Spa an Architectural Heritage Award from the Urban Redevelopment Authority in 2005.

The unique tropical garden spa concept brings the experience outdoors as well as in, drawing on nature and the positive life energy of plants and water to create a truly healing environment. Guests are encouraged to arrive early before their appointment to enjoy the amenities in this 6,000-sq m

(64,583-sq ft) paradise: the mud pools' volcanic mud can be applied to purify the skin; two labyrinths provide space for solitary reflective walks; and the serene landscaped gardens are ideal spots for meditation. They are also welcome to linger after their treatment to maximise its therapeutic effect.

State-of-the-art facilities such as Galaxy Steam Baths and Vichy showers complement the pampering options in the luxurious spa menu. With thermotherapy and hydrotherapy treatments, lulurs (Javanese wedding treatments), massages, body contouring, facials, manicures and pedicures, scalp treatments, scrubs and wraps, guests will be spoilt for choice. Some of the popular local offerings include the Rooibos Face and Body Anti-Ageing Delight, Tropical Glow and Singapore Flower Ritual. Carefully planned day

THIS PAGE (FROM LEFT): The float pool with cascading waterfall is just one of the many amenities guests can enjoy; meditation in the labyrinth helps clear the mind; outdoor spa bath in the Spa Pavilion.

OPPOSITE (FROM LEFT): The relaxing Galaxy Steam Bath is adapted from old Asian and Middle Eastern cleansing rituals; a soothing floral bath in the Japanese Tub.

packages combine different therapies with healthy meals for a complete wellness experience. There are also specialised treatments such as the 2½-hour Five Elements Cleanse and Purify Ritual, a detoxifying regimen of Tibetan and Chinese medicine origins that uses ginseng and lotus blossom.

The private suites offer the most exclusive spa options. The Spa Botanica Suite comes with a private outdoor deck, spacious relaxation areas and a whirlpool. The Royal Suite comes with the King's Bath,

a 450-kg (992-lb) hand-tooled cast bronze tub that retains the warmth of sensuous milk, floral or herbal baths. Guests can also participate in relaxation activities such as swimming, or sign up for a variety of fitness and movement classes.

Fresh juices, fragrant herbal teas and light snacks are available at the Juice Bar, which has a Natural Indulgence juice menu especially for the health-conscious. The Terrace, the resort's all-day dining restaurant, serves healthy spa cuisine. Those who want to bring the Spa Botanica experience home can choose from the range of products at the Spa Shop.

In 2005, The Sentosa Resort & Spa was awarded 'Best Spa' by Small Luxury Hotels of the World and 'Singapore's Leading Spa Resort' by World Travel Awards. It also won the Singapore Tourism Awards' 'Best Spa Experience' from 2003 to 2005, establishing its position as a premier holistic wellness retreat.

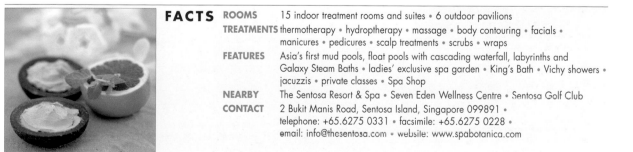

FACTS	**ROOMS**	15 indoor treatment rooms and suites • 6 outdoor pavilions
	TREATMENTS	thermotherapy • hydroptherapy • massage • body contouring • facials • manicures • pedicures • scalp treatments • scrubs • wraps
	FEATURES	Asia's first mud pools, float pools with cascading waterfall, labyrinths and Galaxy Steam Baths • ladies' exclusive spa garden • King's Bath • Vichy showers • jacuzzis • private classes • Spa Shop
	NEARBY	The Sentosa Resort & Spa • Seven Eden Wellness Centre • Sentosa Golf Club
	CONTACT	2 Bukit Manis Road, Sentosa Island, Singapore 099891 • telephone: +65.6275 0331 • facsimile: +65.6275 0228 • email: info@thesentosa.com • website: www.spabotanica.com

PHOTOGRAPHS COURTESY OF SPA BOTANICA AT THE SENTOSA RESORT + SPA.

Corduroy + Finch

has two Michelin stars to his name, promises are cheaper than any other delicatessen. His "food aquarium", a see-through space with glass walls located next to the bustling deli workstation, contains fresh produce and paté. Freshly baked crusty bread is also available to go with the pate or ham. In the weekends, corduroy&finch's loyal clientele queue even before opening hours just for its breakfast menu.

corduroy&finch's dining area is designed to appeal to the yuppie crowd: the interiors have custom-made furnishings and lights from Italy and Germany; couches and seats are upholstered in corduroy—obviously from which the establishment gets half its name; plates signed by Andy Warhol and Bridget Bardot poster grace the walls; and the raw brick and exposed ventilation shaft provide an industrial look. A wall shelf containing

The old street lamp at the corner of the street marks the spot where people stop for gourmet food. Opened in April 2005 by international hoteliers Murray Aitken, Ralf Spika, Adrian Wong and Loh Lik Peng, corduroy&finch is a café, deli and lounge that offers hearty continental European fare, light Mediterranean delights, daily specials, desserts and pastries.

Discerning gourmands can buy homemade items such as bread, chilli oils and paté at prices which chef Spika, who

...loyal clientele queue even before opening hours just for its breakfast menu.

from the wine list. In the evenings, Charlie Chaplin and old movies up to the early eighties are projected on a video screen. The establishment provides not just a place for dining, but also a venue for enjoying the company of friends.

The otherwise plain shophouse corduroy&finch occupies has been transformed to a chic establishment thanks to its co-owners and operators.

corduroy&finch provides complimentary valet parking services.

European groceries and produce—all for sale—provide a striking contrast, as do the homey old copper kitchenware and coffee press with quaint handles on display.

The kitchen has displays of caviar tins, lobsters, wooden boxes of farm cheese, as well as red tomatoes and shiny, purple aubergines in wicker baskets. Apart from these ingredients, which are all for sale, corduroy&finch also carries 25-year-old balsamic vinegar, olives and other goodies such as handcrafted chocolate.

Providing perfect accompaniment to meals are international red and white wines

FACTS	**SEATS**	88
	FOOD	continental European
	DRINK	Old and New World wines • cocktails • imported ales and beers
	FEATURES	wine cellar • loft • delicatessen • food aquarium
	NEARBY	Sixth Avenue • King Albert Park
	CONTACT	779 Bukit Timah Road, Singapore 269758 • telephone: +65.6762 0131 • facsimile: +65.6463 8039 • email: info@corduroyandfinch.com • website: www.corduroylifestyle.com

PHOTOGRAPHS COURTESY OF CORDUROY + FINCH.

Il Lido Italian Dining + Lounge Bar

From its hilltop perch within Sentosa Golf Club, Il Lido overlooks the South China Sea. It is flanked by the verdant hills of the golf course with the city as backdrop, creating a veritable palette for all the senses.

Owner Beppe De Vito, creator of the renowned Garibaldi Group of Restaurants, had the inspiration to create a space where tradition merges with modernity.

Il Lido blends traditional Italian cuisine with contemporary aesthetics. The restaurant's 604 sq m (6,500 sq ft) of space embraces an eclectic mix of Italian designer furniture carefully selected for their distinctive style, uniqueness and utilitarian function.

In the chic dining room, with furnishings by the likes of Antonio Citterio, Arne Jacobsen and the Castiglioni Brothers, minimalist lines accentuate the light and fluidity flowing from the al fresco area. Floor to ceiling windows frame the changing hues of an ocean panorama.

In the Lounge Bar, the organic shapes of Perspex Kartell footstools sit in contrast to the sharp geometry of the Piero Lissoni lounges. The illuminated bar creates a play of light and shadow, drawing the eye high above to where Marcel Wanders 'Zepplin' chandelier suspends motionless, an astounding artwork of sprayed fibreglass and metal. Cool, piped in music mixed by local guru X 'Ho enhance the overall ambience.

Award-winning Chef de Cuisine Michele Pavanellos' creations reflect a reverence for tradition in the simple yet perfectly executed classical Italian cuisine.

THIS PAGE (FROM TOP): The designer décor in the Lounge Bar is elegant yet modern; the dining room, like the cuisine, blends the classical and the contemporary.

OPPOSITE (FROM TOP): Like this appetising sea bass, the deceptive simplicity of the food showcases the skills the restaurant's highly trained chef; the al fresco area offers unparalleled views of the straits.

...a reverence for tradition in the simple yet perfectly executed classical Italian cuisine.

With over 20 years experience in some of the finest establishments, including Antica Locanda in Venice, Bice London and The Palace of the Lost City, Michele has also worked alongside Michelin-starred chefs Gualtiero Marchesi and Stefania Moroni.

With emphasis on fresh homemade pasta, seasonal specialties flown in from around the world, fresh seafood and game, the menu satisfies even the most discerning palate. To bring out these exquisite flavours, Il Lido has an impressive wine selection of over 400 labels spanning the old and new world. Its sommelier has ambitions to grow this to over 500, making for one of Singapore's most exclusive wine and champagne selections.

Il Lido provides the quintessential dining experience for the connoisseur, with the attentiveness from management and staff adding a personal touch. The restaurant, which takes its name from Lido island in Venice, is open from 11.00 am to 1.00 am. It is located in Sentosa, Singapore's popular island resort and prime leisure destination.

Nearby attractions include Underwater World, Dolphin Lagoon and Fort Siloso, to name a few. A short ride away over the causeway is Harbourfront and the city.

FACTS

SEATS	restaurant: 120 indoor, 80 outdoor • bar: 50 indoor, 50 outdoor
FOOD	classical regional Italian
DRINK	exclusive Italian wines • Old and New World wines • cocktails
FEATURES	al fresco dining area • à la carte and gourmet menus
NEARBY	Underwater World • Dolphin Lagoon • Fort Siloso
CONTACT	Sentosa Golf Club, 27 Bukit Manis Road #02-00, Sentosa, Singapore 099892 • telephone: +65.6866 1977 • facsimile: +65.6866 1979 • email: beppe@il-lido.com • website: www.il-lido.com

PHOTOGRAPHS COURTESY OF IL LIDO ITALIAN DINING + LOUNGE BAR.

Michelangelo's Restaurant

Michelangelo's is the flagship of Angelo Sanelli's highly successful Michelangelo's group of restaurants. Located in the expatriate enclave of Holland Village, it is adjacent to Sistina Ristorante, Original Sin and Bentfork Cooking School. These establishments all belong under the restaurant group, which also includes Zambuca Italian Restaurant and Bar at the Pan Pacific Hotel.

The restaurant strikes a delicate balance between fine dining and a comfortable, inviting atmosphere. The walls and ceilings feature reproductions of works by the Italian master, and the main dining area is softly lit with candles, providing an intimate and cosy ambience. Al fresco seating is available for patrons who prefer to dine outdoors.

The menu of Chef Angelo and Executive Chef David Warren puts an innovative spin on Italian cuisine, balancing traditional elements with Asian spices to create a provocative array of selections. Aside from grills, healthy salads and unique appetisers, the restaurant is known for its wide selection of pastas. Signature pasta dishes include Vongole Ancona, with live clams simmered in white wine and fresh herbs and served with angel hair pasta and fresh tomato concasse; and Fettucine Tandoor, which marries tandoor-spiced chicken slices with fettucine in a spicy tomato sauce. Chef's specials are also created daily. Servings are generous and some pastas and appetisers can be shared by two.

The restaurant's award-winning wine selection has over 2,300 labels to suit every taste and price range. Like its sister restaurants, it too has won the prestigious *Wine Spectator Magazine* award of excellence and several wine awards, consistently gaining recognition from 1996 to 2006.

The restaurant provides catering services, and can accommodate special events, intimate dinner parties and wedding receptions. It can also be booked for corporate functions, wine tastings, product launches and press events. Michelangelo's prides itself in being able to offer a range of cuisines, including French, Greek and Indian. It also offers a unique and valuable service: an

...an innovative spin on Italian cuisine, balancing traditional elements with Asian spices...

exclusive menu created to cater for the special needs of diabetics without sacrificing taste or quality. Michelangelo's has consistently been chosen among Singapore's Top Restaurants by *Wine and Dine Magazine*, *Tatler Magazine's* Top 100 Restaurants and has also clinched the Excellent Food Award from *Food and Entertainment Magazine*. Culinary director and co-owner Angelo Sanelli, an Australian native of Italian descent, is one of Singapore's leading players in the restaurant industry. He has won *Wine and Dine Magazine's* 'Restaurateur of the Year' award several times since 1998, and his group has more than 120 awards to date. Cooking classes by Michelangelo's are held at Bentfork Cooking School at Blk 43 #01-64 Jalan Merah Saga, Chip Bee Gardens, Singapore 278115.

FACTS

SEATS	dining area: 50 al fresco area: 50
FOOD	contemporary Italian
DRINK	extensive wine list
FEATURES	al fresco seating • chef's specials • special menu for diabetics that can also be catered to vegetarians • open kitchen • catering
NEARBY	Chip Bee Gardens • Holland Road Shopping Centre • souvenir shops • art galleries • antique shops
CONTACT	Blk 44 #01-60 Jalan Merah Saga, Chip Bee Gardens, Holland Village, Singapore • telephone: +65.6475 9069 (Michelangelo's), +65.6475 4961 (Bentfork Cooking School) • facsimile: +65.6475 4319 • email: reservations@michelangelos.com.sg, info@bentfork.sg • websites: www.michelangelos.com.sg, www.bentfork.sg

PHOTOGRAPHS COURTESY OF MICHELANGELO'S RESTAURANT.

One Rochester

One Rochester brings together elements of Old World charm within the tropical fecundity of Rochester Park. This 1930s historical black and white bungalow has been wonderfully restored to provide patrons with an idyllic venue to enjoy drinks and unwind.

Once the stately home of British officers, One Rochester now houses six areas styled after the living spaces of a comfortable, chic home and is the first bar in Singapore with a non-smoking indoor area.

The Living Room with its cosy sofas and warm lamp lighting provide a casual atmosphere of relaxation. A sense of intimacy pervades The Playroom with its sheer curtains and sunken area, whilst The Bar provides guests with an extensive selection of over 200 Old and New World wines, premium beers and cocktails.

In one corner of The Library, brown leather chesterfields and deep burgundy drapes pay homage to One Rochester's colonial past whilst in the other corner, pale wallpaper and delicate chandeliers provide a fresh contrasting style of French chic.

From The Library to The Balcony, One Rochester takes the meaning of al fresco

THIS PAGE: *Meet and enjoy drinks in a setting that is as warm and cosy as a home.*

OPPOSITE: *Guests can soak in the sunset and enjoy the beauty of the evening in this lush setting.*

One Rochester...is fast becoming one of the hottest dining and lifestyle spots in town.

entertainment sessions, from wine tastings to fashion parties that feature guest DJs. Open from 6.00 pm from Mondays to Saturdays, and 9.00 am on Sundays, One Rochester is situated in the heritage area of Rochester Park and is fast becoming one of the hottest dining and lifestyle spots in town.

Places of interest nearby include the cooking studio, Workloft@Wessex, and Holland Village, which boasts a bohemian mix of cafes, galleries, restaurants and bars.

to another level. This second storey deck with its sleek rattan armchairs provide a comfortable perch where patrons can converge over drinks, admire the sunset and activity in the lush garden below.

In The Garden, pathways neatly intersect, connecting to cosy seating nooks and sheltered cabanas secreted amongst palm fronds and exotic flora. High above, the boughs of old trees spread over this private enclave. The soothing sound of water mingles with lounge music and the soft laughter of guests. The temperature in this outdoor setting is controlled so that it is always cool and comfortable.

One Rochester serves a creative selection of tapas and canapés that have an Asian twist. House specialties include Breaded Shitake Mushrooms served with truffle oil-infused mayo, Sinful Pork Crackles, Smoked Salmon Frittatas and Rochester Spiced Potatoes. Traditional English breakfast is served on Sundays. One Rochester also hosts a variety of music and

FACTS

SEATS	220
FOOD	tapas & canapés • traditional English Breakfast on Sundays
DRINK	extensive Old and New World wines • premium Beer • cocktails
FEATURES	6 themed lounge/seating areas • non smoking indoor area
NEARBY	Rochester Park, Holland Village, Science Park
CONTACT	1 Rochester Park, Singapore 139212 • telephone: +65.6773 0070 • facsimile: +65.6775 9477 • email: info@onerochester.com • website: www.onerochester.com

PHOTOGRAPHS COURTESY OF ONE ROCHESTER.

Original Sin Mediterranean Restaurant

Original Sin, which opened in 1997, is Singapore's first Mediterranean vegetarian restaurant. Culinary Director and co-owner Marisa Bertocchi, herself a vegetarian, is an Australian of Italian descent who has lived in Singapore for over 10 years. The former Visual Arts graduate created the impressive mosaic mirror that adorns the dining area.

By day, the open style kitchen, rustic terracotta floors, rich wall colours and natural light create a vibrant ambience. Soft candlelit interiors in warm, earthy tones make dining at night a cosy and intimate

experience. Guests can also choose to dine outdoors, where there is a view of the lively tree-lined street.

But the real focus here is the food. Original Sin's unique meatless menu features innovative interpretations of Mediterranean cuisine and fresh salads with an array of tantalising ingredients. House favourites include the Mezze, Middle Eastern Dip Platter, Moroccan Eggplant, Ricotta Cake, Porcini Polenta and Whole Stuffed Portobello Mushroom. Other standard Mediterranean fare like moussaka, pastas and risotto dishes

...adapts its diverse cuisine to accommodate the guests' varied dietary requests.

are on offer, as are pizzas loaded with interesting toppings. With the focus on the individual, the restaurant adapts its diverse cuisine to accommodate the guests' varied dietary requests. Portions are generous and only the freshest ingredients are used to create the enticing flavours and aromas of its unique dishes.

Original Sin has been chosen as one of Singapore's best restaurants by the prestigious *Wine and Dine Magazine* and *Tatler Magazine*. It has also won the Singapore Promising Brand award in 2005.

The restaurant has an impressive list of wines. It shares wine stock with its sister restaurants under the Michelangelo's restaurant group and like them, it too has won international acclaim and awards such as the *Wine Spectator* award for its varied and superb selection. Some of the finest labels from Australia, USA, Spain, Argentina, Chile, Italy and France are represented; there is something to complement every taste and budget.

The restaurant is located in Holland Village, Singapore's main expatriate enclave. It is close to shopping, pubs, and other dining and entertainment establishments that cater to both locals and foreigners.

Cooking classes by Original Sin are available at Bentfork Cooking School located at Blk 43 #01-64 Jalan Merah Saga in Chip Bee Gardens.

THIS PAGE *(FROM LEFT):* **The Lentil Tower** combines lentils, char-grilled eggplant, roasted capsicum, cherry tomatoes, mesclun and char-grilled Haloumi cheese; arugula sandwiched between spinach, feta and tofu patties.

OPPOSITE *(FROM TOP):* The robust aroma of the **affogato** gives an after-dinner boost; the centrepiece of the vibrant interior is a large mosaic mirror created by Marisa Bertocchi.

FACTS		
	SEATS	dining area: 50 • al fresco: 45
	FOOD	Mediterranean vegetarian
	DRINK	extensive wine list
	FEATURES	open kitchen • al fresco dining • catering for special events
	NEARBY	Chip Bee Gardens • Holland Road Shopping Centre • Holland V Shopping Mall • art galleries and antique shops
	CONTACT	Blk 43 #01-62 Jalan Merah Saga, Chip Bee Gardens, Holland Village, Singapore 278115 • telephone: +65.6475 5605 (Original Sin), +65.6475 4961 (Bentfork Cooking School) • facsimile: +65.6475 4416 • email: reservations@originalsin.com.sg, info@bentfork.sg • websites: www.originalsin.com.sg, www.bentfork.sg

PHOTOGRAPHS COURTESY OF ORIGINAL SIN MEDITERRANEAN RESTAURANT.

Vansh

Vansh (pronounced 'varn-ch') is an exciting Indian dining experience with a unique concept. An offshoot of Rang Mahal restaurant, an award-winning Indian fine dining restaurant located at Pan Pacific Singapore, Vansh means "new generation within the family" in Hindi.

Vansh is more than just a dining venue. It actively engages the diner to fashion an unforgettable experience for himself, one which entails surrendering to a New Age Indian experience. The event begins with the restaurant interiors. Swathed in passionate purples and reds, the décor is unlike any typical Indian restaurant. Curved benches set in recessed coves; artful lighting and a spotlighted open-concept kitchen complete the interior layout, which is innovative, aesthetically pleasing and bold.

The lounge-like environment induces a feeling of peace and tranquillity, encouraging diners to sit back, unwind and enjoy the ambience with a pre-dinner drink such as a mocktail, cocktail or wine.

The wafting aromas from the open kitchen in the middle of Vansh serve as a

THIS PAGE (FROM TOP): Indian food is given a modern twist in both preparation and presentation; the open-concept kitchen provides nightly entertainment with the sounds and smells of chefs at work.

OPPOSITE: Modern design with clean lines coupled with sensuous colours such as red and purple work to further enhance the fiery passion induced by Indian cuisine.

constant reminder that great food is being prepared and served. The authentic Indian fare at the restaurant depicts influences from the country's northern, southern and coastal areas. While curries usually dominate menus at other Indian eateries, the menu at Vansh focuses on tava (griddle) and tandoori fare.

Menu items include Sun-dried Tomato Kulzza, the chef's secret leavened bread, topped with sweet honey and sundried tomatoes, and Malai Murg Tikka, tender chicken enhanced by cashew nut paste.

Orders come in bite-sized portions so diners can taste a wide variety of flavours in one sitting. All dishes are prepared fresh, using top-grade spices and ingredients flown in from India. Olive and vegetable oils are used predominantly. Diners can look forward to a sumptuous Indian feast doused with modern flair—a gastronomic spread and a visual treat each time they visit Vansh.

A newly opened Vansh is in the Feast Village of Starhill Gallery, in Kuala Lumpur.

FACTS

SEATS	interior: 70 • al fresco: 28
FOOD	modern Indian • vegetarian options available
DRINK	extensive wine list
FEATURES	available for private functions
NEARBY	Singapore Indoor Stadium • weekend waterfront bazaar • National Stadium
CONTACT	Stadium Waterfront, 2 Stadium Walk, Singapore Indoor Stadium, Singapore 397691 • telephone: +65.6345 4466 • facsimile: +65.6344 5344 • email: vansh@hind.com.sg • website: www.vansh.com.sg

Asiatique Collections

Asiatique Collections is the brainchild of Chin Chelliah Bottinelli, who has scoured Asia to collect and produce furniture and decorative items that complement both traditional Asian and minimalist homes.

The Dempsey community where Asiatique is located is five minutes from the busy Orchard Road shopping belt. The lush, green surrounds provide the perfect backdrop for the shop's contemporary Asian style. Asiatique has been here for 10 years, and has grown together with the Dempsey estate.

What began as Chin's small hobby-cum-business selling little chests, lamps, candles and fabric has slowly grown into a double showroom exhibiting Asian furniture and art. One of the first things people notice is the soothing aromatherapy that greets them as they walk in, a prelude to a pleasant and satisfying shopping experience.

The front showroom contains Asiatique's signature teak furniture, which are designed in Singapore and manufactured in Indonesia. There are, amongst other things, day beds, dining sets, bed frames and mirrors. There are pieces in art deco as well as more adventurous styles, but all share a common minimalist theme. The lamps, which are the shop favourites, come in various fabrics and colours that create different moods.

The showroom at the back houses furniture and accessories from China and Thailand, which are designed in collaboration with indigenous craftsmen with whom Chin

THIS PAGE: *The teak furniture Chin Chelliah Bottinelli designs is manufactured in Indonesia.*

OPPOSITE: *Every piece is something Chin would personally endorse.*

...complement both traditional Asian and minimalist contemporary homes.

is frequently in contact. There are red Chinese dressers, low and wide coffee tables, complete dining table sets, light brown bamboo chests, stark black cupboards—and an array of colours, shapes, textures and themes with which to experiment.

Chin travels on a regular basis to acquire new pieces for her large collection, which is on average updated with a shipment of the latest acquisitions every month. She never sells anything that she would not buy for herself—something that is appreciated by the people who share her taste.

Clients can shop comfortably in this pleasant environment, where acquiring only one item is as satisfying a transaction as committing the interior of one's home to Asiatique's care. They can pick up tips on how to match various pieces, taking into account what their homes already have. Chin frequently moves objects around the showroom to help clients visualise the same piece in different settings. The expertly trained staff who help clients beautify their homes know their products well. They can enumerate information about them as readily as they can discuss their origin and tips on maintenance.

Asiatique caters to a good mix of clients. It also works directly with designers, architects and overseas buyers in executing design concepts for homes and other interiors. It custom-makes items for those with specific needs, and also offers its products for export.

FACTS

PRODUCTS	furniture • artwork • home accessories • lamps • tableware • aromatherapy • bedding • soft furnishings • jewellery
FEATURES	customised design • interior design • projects • shipping services
NEARBY	wine merchants • restaurants • shops
CONTACT	Block 14-5 Dempsey Road, Singapore 249675 • telephone: +65.6471 3146 • facsimile: +65.6471 0786 • email: sales@asiatiquecollections.com

PHOTOGRAPHS COURTESY OF ASIATIQUE COLLECTIONS.

Galerie Cho Lon

One distinctive feature of Galerie Cho Lon is that it is never the same. What you spotted only yesterday and had every intention of bringing home today may no longer be there. Because items are in limited quantities, a smart buyer is one who leaves the store a proud owner. New items are added all the time, so it is a good idea to pay frequent visits and check out the latest arrivals.

Cho Lon, which means 'marketplace' in Vietnamese (and is the old name for Saigon's Chinatown), is conceptualised as a home store with an extensive range of goods. It caters to a niche market of collectors—people who appreciate the fascinating mix of old and new, traditional and eclectic, classic and quirky. Cho Lon's Ros Lovell, an ardent collector of interesting discoveries from all over the world, has turned her 20-year passion into a dynamic business. Her store is filled with curios and curiosities from Asia and Europe—from antique furniture to battered leather trunks, cabinets, gilded mirrors, old shoe horns, walking sticks with beautiful silver filigree handles and silk slippers.

Lovell acquires whatever tickles her fancy, but the owner of Galerie Cho Lon also has a keen eye and knows exactly what her customers want. Items span the gamut of old globes, wooden pond yachts, original Minim desks with bone inlay and iconic, hand-built Anglepoise desk lamps, which are exclusive to her store. There are interesting conversation pieces in this shop full of whimsy, such as a

THIS PAGE: Small objects that speak volumes not only about where they came from, but also about their owner's personal tastes.

OPPOSITE: Finding the perfect piece to bring home is like going on a treasure hunt.

...filled with curios and curiosities from Asia and Europe...

reconditioned Saigon barber's chair, hanging bird cages, jewellery reminiscent of the 1920s and original glass decanters. Carr's historical country maps stand in their own section, as do glasses with engraved lead crystal.

There are over 2,000 different book and CD titles available, even though Galerie Cho Lon is a home store. One can find extraordinary titles like *Instructions for British Servicemen in France 1944*, *Poetry for Cats* and even a wide range of children's classics such as *Swallows and Amazons* and *Struwwelpeter*. An active book club has sprung from the store's regulars. Its members can request titles for the shop to acquire and then snap them up the moment they arrive.

The diverse range of items available make the store a great source for one-of-a-kind gifts. Apart from original furniture, unusual lighting and a unique collection of books and recordings, Galerie Cho Lon also retails contemporary pieces and modern home accessories.

FACTS	**PRODUCTS**	curios • antique and contemporary furniture • old and new home accessories • unusual books and recordings • gifts • original and contemporary lamps
	FEATURES	shipping services • free home delivery for purchases above S$500 • gift wrapping service • book club
	NEARBY	Holland Village • shopping • bars and restaurants • spas
	CONTACT	43 Jalan Merah Saga #01-76 & 78, Singapore 278115 • telephone: +65.6473 7922 • facsimile: +65.6276 6574 • email: info@cho-lon.com

PHOTOGRAPHS COURTESY OF GALERIE CHO LON.

John Erdos Gallery

The John Erdos Gallery is known for creating beautiful, expressive furniture made from the finest reclaimed teak from Indonesia. It is contemporary, but with a respect for tradition. Each piece speaks volumes—not just about the tradition of craftsmanship behind it, but also about the person who chooses it to grace his home.

The gallery's three-storey space highlights a wide variety of items in four distinct styles. The Raffles line is inspired by the Dutch colonial period in Indonesia, and features traditional hand-carving. The Loft collection offers more contemporary pieces with touches of the traditional. The Studio Collection is inspired by the lines and high quality materials of the Arts and Crafts period. The Empire Collection is subtle, chic, streamlined and sleek. It draws its inspiration from design trends of the 1940s and 1950s. The East Hampton Collection launched in April 2006 features furniture that embodies indoor-outdoor living.

The gallery carries exquisite four-poster beds, elegant dining tables, cabinets, screens and coffee tables. The comfortable sofas can be turned into the centrepiece of the living space. There are also other home accessories that enhance comfort, provide practical storage solutions and add character and interest to any home.

John Erdos designs all the collections himself, and each piece is made at his factory and workshop in Central Java. John, who started the gallery in 1991 after moving to Singapore from New York, describes his furniture as "strong, good-looking and friendly". His design philosophy—comfortable, practical furniture made with the finest materials and finishes.

...known for creating beautiful, expressive furniture made from the finest teak...

In New York, John's celebrity clientele has included actresses Susan Sarandon and Julia Roberts as well as designers Donna Karan and Giorgio Armani.

Located in a thriving artistic and entertainment district, the gallery is bordered by the bustling dining and night life scene of Mohamed Sultan Road, and the more laid-back residential and commercial River Valley area. The 3,352-sq m (11,000-sq ft) gallery is housed in two adjoining four-storey shophouses designed by renowned architect Richard Ho. The space was chosen for its historical significance and uniquely Singaporean character.

At the heart of the gallery is an open-air water courtyard which allows natural light to stream into each of the building's rooms. The gallery has more than fifteen rooms—each styled to show customers what the furniture would look like in a real home. The project won a Singapore Institute of Architects Design Award in 2001.

PHOTOGRAPHS COURTESY OF JOHN ERDOS GALLERY.

FACTS

PRODUCTS high quality teak wood furniture • home accessories • lamps and lighting • gifts
FEATURES custom-made furniture
NEARBY shopping • fine art galleries • dining and night life • sightseeing • city tours • cinemas
CONTACT 83 Kim Yam Road, Singapore 239378 • telephone: +65.6735 3307 • facsimile: +65.6735 5132 • email: info@johnerdosgallery.com. • website: www.johnerdosgallery.com

index

Numbers in *italics* denote pages where pictures appear. Numbers in **bold** denote map pages.

index

picturecredits

directory

Saint Pierre The Restaurant (page 150)
3 Magazine Road
#01-01 Central Mall
Singapore 059570
telephone : +65.6438 0887
facsimile : +65.6438 4887
edina@saintpierre.com.sg
www.saintpierre.com.sg

San Marco The Restaurant (page 152)
1 Fullerton Square
#08-00 The Fullerton Singapore
Singapore 049178
telephone : +65.6438 4404
facsimile : +65.6438 4424
info@sanmarco.com.sg
www.sanmarco.com.sg

Senso Ristorante + Bar (page 182)
21 Club Street
Singapore 069410
telephone : +65.6224 3534
facsimile : +65.6224 5508
senso@signet.com.sg
www.senso.sg

Vansh (page 220)
2 Stadium Walk, Stadium Waterfront
Singapore Indoor Stadium
Singapore 397691
telephone : +65.6345 4466
facsimile : +65.6344 5344
vansh@hind.com.sg
www.vansh.com.sg

Whitebait + Kale (page 66)
1 Orchard Boulevard
Camden Centre #01-01
Singapore 248649
telephone : +65.6333 8697
facsimile : +65.6333 8035
marcom@whitebaitandkale.com
www.whitebaitandkale.com

Zambuca Italian Restaurant + Bar (page 154)
7 Raffles Boulevard
#03-00 Pan Pacific Singapore
Singapore 039595
telephone : +65.6337 8086
         (Zambuca)
         +65.6475 4961
         (Bentfork Cooking School)
facsimile : +65.6336 8494
reservations@zambuca.com.sg
info@bentfork.sg
www.zambuca.com.sg, www.bentfork.sg

Bars

Beaujolais Wine Bar (page 184)
1 Ann Siang Hill
Singapore 069784
telephone : +65.6224 2227
facsimile : +65.6324 4787
beaujolais@mac.com

W Wine Bar (page 186)
11 Club Street
Singapore 069405
telephone : +65.6223 3886
facsimile : +65.6223 5233
gina@senso.com.sg
www.wwinebar.sg

Shops

Aliya (page 70)
290 Orchard Road
#03-47 The Paragon
Singapore 238859
telephone : +65.6836 1403

252 North Bridge Road
#02-21 Raffles City Shopping Centre
Singapore 179103
telephone : +65.6339 3186
aliya@pacific.net.sg
www.aliyastore.com

Asiatique Collections (page 222)
Block 14-5 Dempsey Road
Singapore 249675
telephone : +65.6471 3146
facsimile : +65.6471 0786
sales@asiatiquecollections.com

The Carat Club (page 74)
15 Emerald Hill Road
Singapore 229297
telephone : +65.6738 1368
facsimile : +65.6235 1389
tccspore@thecaratclub.com
www.thecaratclub.com

Club 21 Gallery (page 76)
190 Orchard Boulevard
#01-07/8 Four Seasons Hotel
Singapore 248646
telephone : +65.6887 5451
facsimile : +65.6735 2993
www.clubtwentyone.com

Felt (page 156)
11 Stamford Road
#01-18 Capitol Building
Singapore 178884
telephone : +65.6837 3393
facsimile : +65.6837 2837
enquires@felt.com.sg
www.felt.com.sg

Galerie Cho Lon (page 224)
43 Jalan Merah Saga #01-76 & 78
Singapore 278115
telephone : +65.6473 7922
facsimile : +65.6276 6574
info@cho-lon.com

HaKaren Art Gallery (page 78)
19 Tanglin Road
#02-43 Tanglin Shopping Centre
Singapore 247909
telephone : +65.6733 3382
facsimile : +65.6735 9709
enquiries@hakaren.com
www.hakaren.com

Jim Thompson (page 80)
390 Orchard Road
Palais Renaissance #01-08 & #02-10
Singapore 238871
telephone: +65.6323 4800

391 Orchard Road
Ngee Ann City B1
Takashimaya
Singapore 238873

25 Scotts Road
DFS Scottswalk Level 1
Singapore 228220

1 Beach Road
Raffles Hotel Arcade #01-07
Singapore 189673
siamsilk@singnet.com.sg

John Erdos Gallery (page 226)
83 Kim Yam Road
Singapore 239378
telephone : +65.6735 3307
facsimile : +65.6735 5132
info@johnerdosgallery.com
www.johnerdosgallery.com

The Link (page 82)
The Link/alldressedup, 333 Orchard Road
#02-01/01-01 Meritus Mandarin
Singapore 238867

The Link Home, 390 Orchard Road
#01-10 Palais Renaissance
Singapore 238871

The Link Wedding, Orange Grove Road
Level 1 Shangri-la
Singapore 258350

The Link bagbar/Etro/Miss Sixty
290 Orchard Road
#01-31/01-30/ 02-29 Paragon
Singapore 238859

Energie
260 Orchard Road
#02-01 The Heeren Shops
Singapore 238855

Miss Sixty
435 Orchard Road
#02-47/47A Wisma Atria
Singapore 238877
telephone : +65.6736 0645
facsimile : +65.6733 7251
www.thelink.sg

Mata-Hari Antiques (page 84)
19 Tanglin Road
#02-26 Tanglin Shopping Centre
Singapore 247909
telephone : +65.6737 6068
facsimile : +65.6738 3579
bernis@singnet.com.sg

Mod.Living (page 158)
331 North Bridge Road
#02-01/08 Odeon Towers
Singapore 188720
telephone : +65.6336 2286
facsimile : +65.6352 7249
enquiries@modliving.com.sg
www.modliving.com.sg

Mumbai Sé (page 86)
390 Orchard Road
#02-03 Palais Renaissance
(opposite Hilton Hotel)
Singapore 238871
telephone : +65.6733 7188
facsimile : +65.6733 6031
pr@mumbai-se.com
www.mumbai-se.com

Rang Mahal (page 146)
7 Raffles Boulevard
Pan Pacific Singapore, Level 3
Marina Square, Singapore 039595
telephone : +65.6333 1788
facsimile : +65.6333 1660
rangmahal@hind.com.sg
www.rangmahal.com.sg

Raoul (page 88)
290 Orchard Road
#02-02/03 and #02-12
Paragon Shopping Centre
Singapore 238859
telephone : +65.6737 0682
         +65.6737 9619

3 Temasek Boulevard
#01-22/24 Suntec City Mall
Singapore 038983
telephone : +65.6883 2589

9 Raffles Boulevard
#01-39/40 Millenia Walk
Singapore 039596
telephone : +65.6837 2748

16 Collyer Quay
#01-11/12 Hitachi Tower
Singapore 049318
telephone : +65.6538 3390

RAOUL Men: Airport Boulevard
Changi Airport, #026-107-01
Terminal 2 Building
Singapore 819643
telephone : +65.6542 9660
www.raoul.com

Risis (page 92)
176 Orchard Road
#01-40 Centrepoint Shopping Centre
Singapore 238843
telephone : +65.6235 0988

3 Temasek Boulevard
Suntec City Mall #01-084
Singapore 038983
telephone : +65.6338 8250

1 Woodlands Square
Causeway Point #01-37
Singapore 738099
telephone : +65.6893 9930

Airport Boulevard
Changi Airport Terminal 1
Departure/Transit Lounge #021-43
Singapore 918141
telephone : +65.6542 0220

RISIS Nature Gallery
Cluny Road, National Orchid Garden
Singapore Botanic Gardens
Singapore 259569
telephone : +65.6835 2492
         +65.6475 5104
clientservice@risis.com.sg
www.risis.com

Tangs (page 94)
310-320 Orchard Road
Singapore 238864
telephone : +65.6737 5500
facsimile : +65.6734 4714
customer_service@tangs.com.sg
www.tangs.com

Vanilla Home (page 188)
48 Club Street
Singapore 069425
telephone : +65.6324 6206
facsimile : +65.6324 6207
contact@vanilla-home.com
www.vanilla-home.com

Wisma Atria (page 98)
435 Orchard Road
Singapore 238877
telephone : +65.6235 2103
facsimile : +65.6733 4037
concierge@macquariepacificstar.com
www.wismaonline.com

Spa

Spa Botanica at The Sentosa Resort + Spa (page
2 Bukit Manis Road
Sentosa Island
Singapore 099891
telephone : +65.6275 0331
facsimile : +65.6275 0228
info@thesentosa.com
www.spabotanica.com